More Praise for *Accidental Genius*

"Mark Levy teaches readers a wonderful mental technology, freewriting, that helps you dive deep into your unconscious to discover treasures, like your next business venture, marketing campaign, or movie script. This book is a must for all who need to reach their most precious assets."
—**B. J. Bueno, founder of The Cult Branding Company and coauthor of** *The Power of Cult Branding*

"One of the best books I've ever read on unlocking your thoughts—your chatter—and turning them into something powerful and meaningful. I'm recommending it to all my clients."
—**Jerry Colonna, cofounder of the venture capital firm Flatiron Partners and executive coach**

"Mark Levy is the creative force behind all my live magic shows, television appearances, newspaper interviews, and even my book. We use the techniques he explains in *Accidental Genius* to explore surprising ways of presenting magic. By following the techniques in this expanded edition of Mark's book, you'll learn how to create your own miracles in whatever realm of life you work."
—**Steve Cohen, "The Millionaires' Magician," cocreator of** *Chamber Magic***, the longest running one-man show in New York City**

"Mark Levy's techniques for breaking the dam to unleash ideas and solutions, words and pages, are brilliant, quirky, and doable. I love this book."
—**Debbie Weil, corporate social media consultant and author of** *The Corporate Blogging Book*

"I devoured the second edition in one sitting, even though I had to pee really badly near the end. Mark made a great book even better. I'll apply what I learned to improve my thinking and writing process starting today."
—**David Meerman Scott, author of** *The New Rules of Marketing & PR*

"*Accidental Genius* can change your life. Really. Mark's ideas will help you open up remarkable 'aha' possibilities for your business, for your writing, and for what you should really being doing with your life."

—**Lois Kelly, author of *Beyond Buzz* and the Dying to Help blog**

"Mark Levy has penned the book that solves the problems all writers and people in general face: they get stuck. Mark does a truly spectacular job of showing you how to unleash genius. Many of these ideas I've used for two decades to author twenty books—I will use them to write my next twenty. This book is a gift for all those who have the desire to share their thoughts with the world—and with themselves."

—**Kevin Hogan, author of *The 168 Hour Week* and *The Psychology of Persuasion***

"When we need to generate content or solve a problem, most of us sit down and think about it. Levy gives us an alternative approach. Rather than laboriously forcing ideas, his process provides a vehicle for thoughts to flow freely. The result? Powerful new ideas and a compelling way of communicating them. The process becomes easy, creative, and enjoyable, enabling us to generate content we can't wait to share."

—**Larina Kase, PsyD, MBA, author of *The Confident Leader* and coauthor of the *New York Times* bestseller *The Confident Speaker***

"Freewriting has become my secret weapon. I use it every day to work my way through problems and find new, creative solutions, to summon wisdom and guidance that I didn't know I had, and to imagine possibilities that once seemed out of reach. I use it with my clients to leverage their inherent knowledge and intelligence to guide them in their businesses. Mark's book does more than get you writing. His exercises and prompts unlock your creative genius. It's straightforward and entertaining, and most importantly it is wildly inspiring. Fasten your seatbelt. Once you start freewriting you don't know where you'll end up—and you'll certainly never go back."

—**Kate Purmal, founder of Kate Purmal Consulting and a former executive with SanDisk and Palm**

"*Accidental Genius* is essential reading for all who want to plumb the depths of their creativity and wisdom—and send their inner editor on vacation. Which should be everybody."

—Lloyd Dangle, cartoonist and author of *Troubletown*

"*Accidental Genius* makes us realize that we squander our greatest asset: our creativity. New businesses, new successes, and new profits never blossom because people let their good ideas die on the vine. Levy deftly teaches how to help your ideas come alive and bloom into books, products, companies, and more. The simple methods in this book bring forth the magic in our minds and show us how to grab it, plant it, cultivate it, and grow something new under the sun."

—Nick Corcodilos, founder of AsktheHeadhunter.com

"Mark Levy's simple yet revolutionary writing tips are about to awaken your genius so you can accomplish the things you want to in life. Your genius is waiting!"

—Thomas Clifford, *Fast Company* "Expert Blogger" and corporate communications producer

"*Accidental Genius* is a work of genius—but not accidental. Mark's wit, wisdom, and world-wise years of hard work are delivered with an eloquent sophistication of simplicity that informs, educates, and entertains. Anyone who reads this will benefit greatly—writers, marketers, PR professionals, business leaders, sales, and more. Buy this book. Read it. Use it. Awaken the genius within."

—Steve Kayser, editor of the online business magazine *Cincom Expert Access*

"Whoever said 'geniuses are born, not made'? Well, I did, until this incredible book! It took Mark Levy not just to tell us all to 'be remarkable' but to show us how! Where were you when I started out twenty-five years ago? Well, at least we've got it now."

—Bill Schley, author of *The Micro-Script Rules* and *Why Johnny Can't Brand*

ACCIDENTAL GENIUS

ACCIDENTAL GENIUS

Using Writing to
Generate Your Best
Ideas, Insight,
and Content

MARK LEVY

BK

Berrett–Koehler Publishers, Inc.
San Francisco
a BK Life book

Berrett-Koehler Publishers, Inc.
235 Montgomery Street, Suite 650
San Francisco, CA 94104-2916
Tel: (415) 288-0260   Fax: (415) 362-2512   www.bkconnection.com

Ordering Information
Quantity sales. Special discounts are available on quantity purchases by corporations, associations, and others. For details, contact the "Special Sales Department" at the Berrett-Koehler address above.
Individual sales. Berrett-Koehler publications are available through most bookstores. They can also be ordered directly from Berrett-Koehler: Tel: (800) 929-2929; Fax: (802) 864-7626; www.bkconnection.com
Orders for college textbook/course adoption use. Please contact Berrett-Koehler: Tel: (800) 929-2929; Fax: (802) 864-7626.
Orders by U.S. trade bookstores and wholesalers. Please contact Ingram Publisher Services, Tel: (800) 509-4887; Fax: (800) 838-1149; E-mail: customer.service@ingrampublisherservices.com; or visit www.ingrampublisherservices.com/Ordering for details about electronic ordering.

Berrett-Koehler and the BK logo are registered trademarks of Berrett-Koehler Publishers, Inc.

Printed in the United States of America

Berrett-Koehler books are printed on long-lasting acid-free paper. When it is available, we choose paper that has been manufactured by environmentally responsible processes. These may include using trees grown in sustainable forests, incorporating recycled paper, minimizing chlorine in bleaching, or recycling the energy produced at the paper mill.

Library of Congress Cataloging-in-Publication Data
Levy, Mark,
  Accidental genius : using writing to generate your best ideas, insights, and content / by Mark Levy. — 2nd ed.
     p. cm.
  Includes bibliographical references.
  ISBN 978-1-60509-525-7 (pbk. : alk. paper)
1. English language—Rhetoric—Problems, exercises, etc.   2. Critical thinking—Problems, exercises, etc.   3. Business writing—Problems, exercises, etc.   I. Title.
  PE1479.B87L48 2010
  808'.042—dc22

                          2010005822

First Edition
15 14 13 12 11 10   10 9 8 7 6 5 4 3 2 1

Text designer: Detta Penna
Copyeditor: Joy Matkowski
Proofreader: Katherine Lee
Indexer: Kirsten Kite

Cover designer: Ian Shimkoviak/The Book Designers
Cover photo: Shutterstock

Contents

The act of writing stimulates thought, so when you cannot think of anything to write, start writing anyway.

Barbara Fine Clouse, *Working It Out: A Troubleshooting Guide for Writers*

Introduction

Your Mind Is Bigger Than You Think

Let's talk about your mind. It holds more than you could imagine in terms of experiences, stories, images, and ideas. Want proof? Just think about all the phenomena that appear in your mind without you willing it there.

Take dreams. You don't command them into being, nor do you steer their surreal content. Yet your dreams emerge from somewhere.

Memories act the same way. You're in the kitchen preparing soup and remember a day from childhood when your family was eating steak. You didn't summon that memory. It showed up on its own.

Other types of thoughts also turn up without help. You're sitting in traffic when the answer to a computer problem hits you. How did that happen? You weren't thinking about the computer problem, but your mind created the thought and somehow pushed it into existence.

INTRODUCTION

Those dreams, memories, and thoughts didn't come from outside of you. You generated them through means hidden from you.

Our minds hold a vast invisible inventory of thoughts and expertise. These phenomena might better help us create ideas and solve problems if we could only reach them, play with them, develop them, and make them practical.

That, then, is what *Accidental Genius* is about: It teaches you how to get at what's inside your head, so you can convert the raw material of your thoughts into something usable, even extraordinary.

How do I propose to help you get to these extraordinary ideas of yours? Through writing. Or, more specifically, through something called freewriting.

Freewriting is one of the most valuable skills I know. It's a way of using your body to get mechanical advantage over your mind, so your mind can do its job better.

As expansive and impressive as the mind is, it's also lazy. Left to its own devices, it recycles tired thoughts, takes rutted paths, and steers clear of unfamiliar and uncomfortable territory. You could say that one of its primary jobs is to shut off, even when there's important thinking to be done.

Freewriting prevents that from happening. It pushes the brain to think longer, deeper, and more unconventionally than it normally would. By giving yourself a handful of liberating freewriting rules to follow, you back your mind into a corner where it can't help but come up with new thoughts. You could call freewriting a form of forced creativity.

This technique will work for you even if you don't consider yourself a gifted writer or thinker. The writing itself generates thought, which is why some refer to this technique as automatic writing. It often produces intriguing results without labored effort on the part of the writer. At times, the thoughts seem to pop up on their own.

How Did I Come across Freewriting?

It was 1995 or so, and I got a call from a friend who edited a local entertainment newspaper. He told me that one of my rock 'n roll heroes, Paul Weller, was coming to perform in nearby New York City, and would I want a free ticket?

Would I! Weller, a Brit, hadn't toured America for years. Who knew when he'd return? Of course I wanted a ticket. The catch? I had to review the concert for my friend's paper.

Writing a concert review might not seem like a big deal, but I hadn't written anything in a decade. Did I still know how to write? Even if I did know, how do you describe music? ("The drum went bum-bum, bum-bum, bum-bum?") Still, I took the assignment.

The concert wasn't happening for a week, so to prepare, I pulled a paperback off my bookshelf that I'd never gotten around to reading, Peter Elbow's *Writing with Power*. Its premise was wild: Even if you thought you were blocked and didn't know what to say, you could produce reams of ideas and words. I had bought the book years earlier, figuring this day would come. You know: In Case of Emergency, Break Glass.

One of *Writing with Power*'s chief techniques was freewriting, which I'd experienced in high school when teachers assigned it as punishment if the class was noisy, or to occupy us when they wanted to go to the teachers' lounge and smoke. I thought of freewriting as hollow busy work.

Elbow's approach to the technique was far different from the one taken by my teachers. To Elbow, freewriting was an all-purpose tool that was a spigot to the deepest part of the mind. It helped you generate words and ideas; write essays, poems, and stories; and access an authorial voice that was honest and thoughtful.

Elbow himself had started using freewriting when he had been blocked for years. Judging from the bulk of

INTRODUCTION

Writing with Power, 384 pages of small type and even smaller footnotes, now he couldn't keep himself from writing. The technique had helped him become a prose geyser. I was inspired.

The concert rolled around and—using freewriting—I wrote it up. My friend the editor gave me more assignments, and I started writing for other media outlets, too. While I worked on these assignments, a funny thing would occur.

I'd be exploring my assigned topic through freewriting and, following the dictates of the technique, I'd digress. Often, my digressions concerned my day job and the problems I experienced as a sales director for a book wholesaler. While I was supposed to be writing a review of a TV show, I'd wander and write about a prospect my company was trying to win. While I was doing a profile on a punk rocker, I'd veer toward ways of coaching a troublesome employee.

In the end, I'd finish my article, but I also frequently came away with answers to my problems in the rest of my life. Accidentally, I was acting as my own consultant.

I was so enamored with the business results the technique was producing that I started searching for a book that would take me further. I found excellent volumes on using freewriting to improve one's prose, but none on using it as a problem-solving tool for business.

Eventually, I decided that if I wanted to know what a book like that would tell me, I'd have to write it. That's when I began work on what would become the original edition of *Accidental Genius*.

That original edition was released in the year 2000. In the time since, I've opened my own strategic marketing and ideation consultancy, and I use freewriting on nearly every project I take on.

How Can Freewriting Help You?

Freewriting is a fast method of thinking onto paper that enables you to reach a level of thinking that's often difficult to attain during the course of a normal business day.

This technique will help you understand your world, spot opportunities and options, solve problems, create ideas, and make decisions. It'll also help you become a better writer, both stylistically and idea-wise.

Throughout the book, I'm going to demonstrate freewriting with business problems as examples—problems concerning strategy, marketing, positioning, sales, business writing, and such. That's just my choice.

In reality, you can use the technique to help you explore situations of all kinds in any field you can imagine, such as world events, politics, science, health, mathematics, urban planning, architecture, engineering, psychology, philosophy, social media, food, entertainment, and sports.

So, if you were trying to figure out ways of structuring a joint venture with a business associate, freewriting could help you. But you could also use it to wrap your head around ways of balancing the state budget, decreasing overcrowding in schools, forming a neighborhood alliance, inventing a video game, writing a blog post, fixing a relationship, planning a party, mapping out a vacation, devising a workout regimen, and developing a recipe.

You could even use freewriting to help you find a purpose when you don't have a purpose in mind.

What you're reading right now is the revised, expanded second edition of *Accidental Genius*. While I was working on this edition, I asked writers and fans of the first edition what freewriting does for them. Here're some of their (paraphrased) answers:

Freewriting...

5

- Clears logjams in the mind
- Brings clarity
- Provides perspective
- Helps you become articulate about yourself and your ideas
- Provides a path to the core of who you are and want to be
- Prompts you to think differently from peers
- Makes you powerful
- Accesses knowledge you'd forgotten
- Enables you to write with an honesty attractive to readers
- Creates empathy for others
- Cuts resistance to thinking and writing
- Pushes you creatively
- Causes a chain reaction of ideas
- Creates ideas no one but you could have had
- Puts you in touch with your freak side
- Gives you something to feel good about
- Gets you high
- Centers and grounds you
- Creates accountability in a way that's easy and ongoing

How Is the Book Structured?

It's divided into sections: this introduction and three additional parts.

In the first part, you'll learn the six secrets to freewriting. In the second part, you'll explore methods of using freewriting to ideate and solve problems. In the third part, you'll discover ways of using freewriting to generate public works, such as blog posts, speeches, and even books.

More about these parts in a moment.

How Is This Revised Edition Different from the Original Edition?

I can think of four ways:

Difference #1. In the original edition, I taught readers "private writing." In this revised edition, I teach "freewriting." The techniques are identical. Why am I changing the terms?

When I wrote the original edition, I was dead set against anyone ever sharing their exploratory writing. Why? I figured if they knew they'd be sharing, they'd alter what they wrote. That means, instead of using their writing to dive into the raw, honest part of the brain, they'd stay on the surface and regurgitate the conventional, inoffensive ideas they were habitually getting.

To make my privacy point, I borrowed a phrase from Peter Elbow and Pat Belanoff and called the technique "private writing." Everything was fine until I started teaching it to clients during my consulting gigs.

We'd be working on their marketplace position or creating a publicity stunt, and I'd ask them to do private writing then and there as a means of shaking up their thinking. I warned them not to show me their work. Instead, they were to use the document as a scratch pad for our conversation.

Despite my request, clients would excitedly read aloud large portions of what they'd written. It happened 100 percent of the time. I can't blame them. They were psyched by what they wrote. More often than not, the ideas they generated were indisputable departures for them, and the language was distinctive. Much of it ended up in their books and keynotes and on their Web sites and social media sites.

Using the phrase "private writing" started making less and less sense. Yeah, the writing starts out as private—and you should absolutely assume that everything you write will remain private and unseen by anyone but you. But once you've used the writing to discover what you're thinking, then it's time to consider going public with some of what you've done.

Hence, a second difference between this edition and the original:

7

Difference #2. This revised edition contains a new section, "Going Public." It's seven chapters and ten thousand-plus words on freewriting-inspired ways of making your ideas and prose public. You could say that this section helps put you on the road to thought leadership, even guruhood. It'll help you use your writing to brainstorm with others and to write books, articles, posts, presentations, and the like. It includes the following chapters:

"Sharing Your Unfinished Thoughts" teaches you the joys of constructing a "talking document" that incorporates your best unrefined writing about some problem you're working on, so you can send it to others for help and conversation. I use talking documents all the time, even when I'm not totally sure about the direction my thinking is taking. At times, just assembling these collage-like documents triggers answers before you even send one out.

"Help Others Do Their Best Thinking" shows how to lead colleagues and clients through freewriting sessions as a way of getting them unstuck and productive.

"Notice Stories Everywhere" calls attention to a phenomenon I spot all the time in other writers: As you start regularly producing pieces for publication—be it for a book, a blog, or whatever—you see the world differently. Everything becomes material for your writing. You think in narrative. The world becomes more interesting, and it seems to make more sense.

"Build an Inventory of Thoughts" explains how I cut my freewriting into thought chunks and then stash those chunks into category-specific documents on my computer. That way, I always have material for future projects. It's kind of a squirrel-and-nut approach to writing.

"Write Your Own Rules" highlights the importance of having a few friendly rules to follow as you write. Doing so gets you to the page faster and keeps you on track once you've gotten there.

"The Fascination Factor" is a favorite of mine. When people want to write a book, they often look to the marketplace first. That approach leads to a boring me-too book. Instead, they should look to the things that have fascinated them throughout life: stories, ideas, observations, movies, and so on. Once they've catalogued that inventory, they can use the material to create a book that's one of a kind and jells with who they are.

"Freewrite Your Way to Finished Prose" starts by looking at how consultant Geoff Bellman approaches book writing through exploratory writing and segues into how I use a combination of freewriting ideas when I'm writing for print.

Difference #3. The revised edition contains seven additional chapters of thinking techniques to use while freewriting:

"Escape Your Own Intelligence" discusses how we can confuse ourselves by trying to use brain-spun abstractions to solve a problem. One solution: List the situation's obvious facts. It's easy and throws your attention into the tangibility of the physical world.

"The Value in Disconnecting" teaches the importance of collecting and evaluating thoughts to use as stepping stones to greater answers.

"Prompt Your Thinking" shows you how to warm up your mind by sending it in unanticipated directions.

"Using Assumptions to Get Unstuck" opens with a surprising story and then discusses ways you can consciously separate yourself from thought barriers.

"Getting a Hundred Ideas Is Easier Than Getting One" talks about how most of us play the "best idea game," when a far more liberating alternative is the "lots of ideas game."

"Learn to Love Lying" is about how to think your way out of a problem whose environment seems closed and unchanging. In such an environment, you need to alter how you're seeing things. Lying to yourself is one way to do this.

You tell a lie about a single factor and then follow the consequences of that lie. From fantasy, you might be able to craft an interesting pragmatic solution.

"The Writing Marathon" discusses how freewriting in sessions of six or seven hours allows you to completely separate from your normal ways of thinking. To do the marathon, you have to start each new session by artificially forcing your mind in a new direction—a hard skill to master made easier through freewriting.

Difference #4. To make room for this new material, I've cut eight chapters from the original text. Those chapters were good, but the ones I swapped them for are better. I've learned a lot in the years between editions.

How Did You Go about Revising a Book You Wrote Ten Years Earlier?

I hadn't planned on revising *Accidental Genius*, but my publisher asked and I thought, Why not? How hard could it be? Most of it had already been written in 1999. Revising it would be like cheating off myself.

They e-mailed me the original manuscript and let me have at it. I opened the file, took a look... and froze.

Staring at all those words made me realize the project's enormity. After days of worry, I decided to move things forward through the best way I know how: freewriting.

I did a bunch of freewriting sessions focusing on what I'd learned about writing and ideation since the book's publication. In particular, I thought about the moments in my consulting practice that woke clients up and helped them do good work. What did I say? What did I do? What did I in turn learn from clients?

Once I had that material, I made a list of all my fascinations (Chapter 27), culled through my "thought chunk" documents (Chapter 25), and added those ideas to the mix. I also interviewed several writers and fans of the first edition, so I'd have additional perspectives and stories to draw on.

I studied all this conceptual inventory and picked out the ideas and techniques I found most valuable. Then I got down to the "real" writing (Chapter 28).

Using a combination of freewriting and conventional writing techniques, I started drafting—in no particular order—chapters. By the time I'd written six or seven new ones, I'd pulled myself back from the ledge.

Having faith in the new material gave me confidence to approach the old. I tweaked some language, cut a handful of chapters that didn't seem as important as I once thought, and added seventeen or so fresh ones.

Thank you, freewriting. I can always count on you. You force me to be creative and productive when I'd rather hide.

Part One

The Six Secrets to Freewriting

We all have an internal editor that cleans up what we're thinking so we can sound smart and in control, and so that we can fit in. This editor helps us live politely among other people, but it hurts our ability to think differently and powerfully.

Freewriting temporarily forces the editor into a subservient role, so you can get to thoughts that are raw, truthful, and unusual. It's from thoughts like these that big ideas are more likely to come.

Here are what I consider the technique's six easy-to-use secrets...

Chapter 1

Secret #1: Try Easy

Robert Kriegel, business consultant and "mental coach" for world-class athletes, tells a story in one of his books that has critical implications for you in your quest to lead a better life through writing.

Kriegel was training a sizable group of sprinters who were battling for the last spots in the Olympic trials. During a practice run, Kriegel found his runners to be "tense and tight"—victims, apparently, of "a bad case of the Gotta's."

Conventional wisdom would have dictated that these highly skilled athletes train harder, but Kriegel had another idea. He asked them to run again, only this time they were to relax their efforts and run at about nine-tenths their normal intensity. Of this second attempt, Kriegel writes:

> The results were amazing! To everyone's surprise, each ran faster the second time, when they were trying "easy." And one runner's time set an unofficial world record.

Fine for running, but does that idea hold for any pursuit? Kriegel continues: "The same is true elsewhere: Trying easy will help you in any area of your life. Conventional Wisdom tells us we have to give no less than 110 percent to keep ahead. Yet conversely, I have found that giving 90 percent is usually more effective."

For freewriting, too, Kriegel's "easy" notion hits the nail on its relaxed head.

Rather than approach your writing with your teeth gritted, demanding instant, virtuoso solutions from yourself, loosen up and ease into your best 90 percent effort. Here's how:

Begin your writing by reminding yourself to try easy. I liken this to the prep work of a baseball player stepping into the batter's box. The player adjusts his batting glove and cup, spits, kicks at the dirt, stares at the barrel of his bat, and eases into a few practice swings. These rituals accomplish two things: They allow the hitter to set up the mechanics of his swing, and they get him in the correct frame of mind to face a pitch.

That's what I'm asking you to do. Get your mechanics down, then do a psych job on yourself. Or, put another way: Start scribbling, then remind yourself that you're simply looking to put some decent words and ideas down on the page; you're not trying to produce deathless prose and world-beating ideas in the course of a single night's writing.

I've opened my computer's freewriting file to find a few examples of how I remind myself to try easy. I don't have to look far.

Nearly every entry begins with a reminder, invocation, plea, entreaty, or declaration of assurance from me to myself to stay centered during the writing and not expect wisdom, insight, or shining prose. Most of the time, I don't specifically say to myself, "Try easy," although the sentiment is there. Here are some samples:

Remove the "Mighty Specialness" of writing, until there's nothing to stop you. This kind of writing is dirt simple, like putting on a sock.

Just some brain-draining, some noodling, going on here. Don't expect lightning bolts.

Okay, a little sticking here to start, like a computer key that hasn't been deep struck for a while. Keep moving and the stickiness may or may not leave, but at least you'll be moving.

Here it is, on the line. I'm squeezing some words onto the page, but I'm scaring myself with demands of originality. If words don't come out of me in interesting arrangements, tasty strings, then my writing fingers slow down, my mind stops. Wait, Mark. That kind of thinking is going to guarantee you no new ideas. Better just forge ahead, and get some stuff onto the page—great or stink-o.

These are hardly inspiring openings, I grant you. But if you, like me, suffer from wanting to accomplish too much, right away, an honest attempt to calm your expectations can improve the quality of your thinking in the long run. You, though, might be wondering, will all this self-reassurance act as an anchor on my thinking and weigh it down far below what is helpful? Might I, in effect, be courting my own dumbness?

The answer is no. Despite your pleas and cautious self-instruction, your mind still begs to solve problems and do extraordinary work. By giving yourself this "try easy" ground rule, you'll ease up on your perfectionistic demands and give your rampaging mind more room to maneuver.

But wait, I have another way—a way virtually guaranteed to move you into that "try easy" zone.

→ Points to Remember

- A relaxed 90 percent is more efficient than a vein-bulging 100 percent effort.
- When you begin freewriting about a thorny subject, remind yourself to "try easy."

Chapter 2

Secret #2: Write Fast and Continuously

That's right: When you write fast and continuously, you pretty much have to adopt an easy, accepting attitude—you don't have much choice.

My assertion—that fast, continuous writing improves thought by relaxing you—needs clarification, though: Just how fast? Just how continuous?

First, just how fast? I'd say about as fast as your hand moves when you scribble a note to your best office buddy, saying "Couldn't wait for you anymore, went to lunch at Giuseppe's," because your colleagues were already piling into a car. You know, fast.

By writing fast, you invite your mind to operate at a pace that's closer to its normal rate of thought, rather than the lethargic crawl you usually subject it to when you write sluggishly.

Here's what I mean, crafted into an experiment: In your

mind, summon up the image of something that happened to you yesterday—a meeting with the boss, a decision you made about the market, whatever. Take pen and paper, and start to write about that image, but write slowly, perhaps at half your normal speed. Spend a few seconds on each word, as your hand traces out the line and curve of each letter. Keep this slowness going for two minutes.

Difficult, isn't it? Did you find, in a sense, that your mind followed your body, that your thinking slowed down to accommodate the snail's pace of your hand? It's almost as if your mind were saying, "Why should I give that situation a good thinking through, if my hand isn't going to have time to record what I'm pondering? Nuts to this." Your mind then either slowed down to match your hand speed, or it wandered off and distracted itself in trivia.

Now do the opposite. Conjure up the same image, but use the next two minutes to get it down on paper twice as fast as you normally would. You needn't push yourself toward bionic speed—just move as quickly as you can without cramping your hand. Try for, say, forty words in a minute. If you want to vary your speed, by all means do, but don't drop back too far. And if you want to talk to yourself on the paper as you're speeding along ("This feels interesting, but awkward"), go ahead and talk.

How was that for a difference? Forget about the quality of your words, and just look at the product of your labor. You've doubtless used ten times the amount of ink, gotten further in your story, and shown more advanced thinking than you did at your slow speed. You may not have done anything impressive yet, but you've demonstrated to yourself, in a small way, that there's a radically different level of thinking going on when you write at a speed closer to the speed of thought.

On to the second question: Just how continuous?

I'd say about as continuous as your grip on the report you spent weeks preparing, only to find out that you didn't address the issue dearest to your CEO's heart. You know, continuous.

> By writing continuously, you force the edit-crazy part of your mind into a subordinate position, so the idea-producing part can keep spitting out words.

What I just wrote is true, but somehow the rich ideas bundled up in that lone sentence need more room to breathe. If your attention inadvertently lagged eight seconds back—maybe your toddler plopped her plate of spaghetti on her head like a hat, or a passing car blared its radio—you'd miss one of the most critical conceptual statements in the book. Here, then, is that same sentence, with its root ideas unbundled, expanded, restated, and dressed up in smart-looking bullet points:

- If your mind knows your hand won't stop moving, it'll ease up on trying to edit out your "inappropriate" and underdeveloped thoughts.

- Normally, your controlling mind censors you because it wants you to look good to yourself and to your public. Now, though, it knows it's been backed into an impossible position; it can't possibly examine your rapidly appearing thoughts for public correctness, so it recedes into the background.

- Your "inappropriate" thoughts are where the action is, and the more quickly you get to them, the more effectively you can fashion solutions for yourself.

- What are "inappropriate" thoughts? They are bone-honest notions you wouldn't normally air in public, things like "I hate my payables department" and "Just for kicks, I wonder what kind of products we would have to invent if we junked our cash cow?" These thoughts, in large part, contain your genius. They're where your originality and distinction reside.

- Your continuous writing acts, in a sense, like a brainstorming session with yourself, but in many ways it's better than traditional brainstorming. While traditional brainstorming asks you to withhold judgment on spontaneously voiced ideas, we all know that's impossible. In public, you can curb your judgment a little, but you can never completely suspend it. In your freewriting, however—since no one but you will likely see it, and your edit-crazy mind is napping—you can access your wildest associations without fear of reprisal.

- Because you have to come up with something to say while you're writing continuously, you stay focused on what you're writing. You know that if you lose your place, you'll have to stop, double back, and pick up the thread of your logic, thus breaking your self-made promise to write continuously. Your normal writing approach doesn't have this Zen-like, stay-in-the-moment focus.

- Continuous writing shows you that individual thoughts are cheap, since you always have new ones following on the heels of current ones. But what if you have to stop because you've run out of things to say? Write meaningless stuff while you wait for your mind to redirect you. That's right: vacuous, senseless, meaningless stuff.

- Babble onto the page: "I went to the hen for twice times two phone drake dreg parala..."

- Repeat the last word you wrote: "The data show show show show show show..."

- Or just repeat the last letter you struck on your keyboard: "The profit I I I I I I I I I I I I I I..."

- Just keep your writing hand revved up and occupied, while your mind quickly considers its options, and then get on to a new thought.

Got it, then? The plan is to move fast and don't stop writing, with the understanding that the more words you pile onto the page, even if they're lousy words, the better your chance at finding a usable idea.

In the freewriting game, think quantity before quality. As sci-fi great Ray Bradbury says about story writing: "You will have to write and put away or burn a lot of material before you get comfortable in the medium." To apply it to freewriting, I'd change this quote to read: "Write with a fast, haphazard hand, because you'll need to burn through all the awful stuff you smear onto the page in order to get to something halfway decent." That's the way to think: The bad brings the good, and there's no way around this natural order.

→ Points to Remember

- If you write as quickly as your hand can move or your fingers can type, and you continue to generate words without stopping, astonishing things will happen. Your mind will eventually give you its grade A, unadulterated thoughts to put on the paper because it realizes it won't be criticized (no one but you will see them), and you might be able to use them (thoughts can be tweaked and developed, once they're on paper).

- If you temporarily run out of things to say, keep your mind and hand in motion by repeating the last word or letter you wrote. You can accomplish the same thing by babbling onto the page in a nonsensical, scat language.

- Your best thought comes embedded in chunks of your worst thought. What's the only way to reliably mine your best thought? Write a lot. Think "quantity." Think "word production." Think of yourself as a word and thought factory.

Chapter 3

Secret #3: Work Against a Limit

Let's apply some of the information you've learned so far. Set your kitchen timer to ring in ten minutes and...

What's that? I haven't yet explained a kitchen timer as a writing aid? Shame on me. Once you start using a timer to help you generate thoughts, you'll never be without one. Your kitchen timer, in fact, will become the most important item on your desk, with your computer running a close second.

Here, then, is why you need the timer: It gives you a time limit against which to conduct your thinking. That's critical, for two reasons:

1. The limit energizes your writing effort by giving you parameters.

Think of it: If I ask you to write fast and continuously about some emotionally charged difficulty you're having at work, how long do you think you could keep the words flowing? Thinking through a tough subject—especially from a variety of angles, as I'll teach you to do—is both exhilarating and exhausting. You can't keep going forever, or even for a short, if indeterminate, amount of time.

See, when I'm asking you to freewrite, I'm asking you to sprint. Now if I specified that you were to sprint flat out for a short, designated distance—say, forty yards—you'd hoof it. But if I implored you to sprint for a vague range— say, between forty yards and forty miles—you'd hold down your speed and wait to see how far you'd have to go. You'd exert yourself less because the parameters of the race were uncertain.

A timer, preset for ten or fifteen minutes, energizes you in your thinking campaign, because it specifically limits the amount of work you have to accomplish in a single bout of writing. Once that timer rings, even if you're in the middle of a sentence, you stop. In a sense, the timer enforces a self-imposed behavioral contract: You promise yourself to think and write deeply for a certain period, you do it, and then you can put your feet up.

2. The limit keeps you writing, so you'll have a chance for a genius moment.

And then there are "those days." On those days when you're brain-dead, or tired, or uninspired, but a presentation is due and you've got to come up with something, your commitment to your timer will keep you writing. True, most of what you produce during this time will be loathsome, but some of it may be usable, or even better than usable.

In the world of freewriting, it's a truism that your freshest notions often come when you've let down your guard and you're writing absolute junk. Call it "try easy," or call it "lowering your expectations," but sometimes your bored or disgusted junk-writing mind redirects you toward places your excited mind bypasses; history is, in fact, full of people who had extraordinary ideas when they were in low, seemingly unproductive, states.

The key, then, is to keep working, even when you're covering your page with babble, and to keep writing until your timer tells you to stop.

That last paragraph would have been a good place to close this chapter, don't you think? If I had quit twenty-odd words back, I would have left you on a high note, with the image of a swiftly writing you shining in your mind, as you tried capturing your own genius moments, no matter what mood you found yourself in.

But if I had stopped there, I would have cheated you out of a small yet significant detail: Buy yourself a timer that doesn't make a clicking noise as it counts down. No wind-up dial timers or dimpled plastic lemons with green numbers running around their circumference that twist in half to activate the timing mechanism. Believe me, you'll thank me for this advice. That clicking noise can be very, very distracting. I thought you should know.

An additional thought: There are, of course, many ways of timing yourself: timers on your watch, your computer, your PDA. But you can also get the same function from your washer or dryer. That's what Chuck Palahniuk, the *Fight Club* author, sometimes does. Before sitting down to write, he throws a load of clothes into one of the machines and then uses its cycle to time his work. So he writes a best seller while doing his chores. There's an extra benefit, says Palahniuk: "Alternating the thoughtful task of writing with the mindless work of laundry or dish washing will give you the breaks you need for new ideas and insights to occur."

→ Points to Remember

- Writing for short, timed periods (normally in the ten- to twenty-minute range) concentrates the mind. Deadlines motivate.
- You needn't feel chipper to have a world-beating thought.

Chapter 4

Secret #4: Write the Way You Think

If you've ever been given advice on how to prepare a document for the business community, you've probably been admonished to "write the way you speak." That is, you've been asked to make your document sound conversational—and, therefore, easier to understand—by using contractions, plain words, personal pronouns, and a dozen minirules to give the impression that you're hovering behind your readers, whispering directly into their ears (although if they tried to shoo you away, there'd be nothing there to swat).

This plain English style of writing is invaluable when you're trying to communicate with others but less valuable for the freewriting page. It's not that the "write the way you speak" tenets are wrong during freewriting, it's that they don't go far enough.

During a bout of freewriting, it's imperative that you get at your raw thoughts before the prissy side of your mind cleans

29

them up for public viewing and, in the process, squelches their effectiveness. So don't "write the way you speak," but "write the way you think." Here's what I mean.

So far, this chapter is written in the kind of language I use when I speak. True, I've edited out lots of "Umms," "You knows?" and other fillers that punctuate my spoken messages. But if you and I had an in-person conversation, you'd certainly recognize me as the same guy who wrote this text, given my vocal cadence, word choices, and expressed thoughts. To you, this Mark-as-writer and Mark-as-speaker would be congruent because in both instances I'm using the same part of my brain that dresses up thoughts for public consumption.

When I write for myself, however, I don't necessarily access this publicly oriented part of my brain. I use the writing solely as a way of watching myself think. Here's an unedited, honest-to-goodness example of a writing session during which my recording hand merely followed the path laid down by my coffee-soaked brain:

> Let's try one with muscle. Lots of useless writing. Abandon the logical edge. This paper will come up from my gurgling stomach, and I'll burp it across the page. Of course, from bleech to finished product often comes out compromised, a provisional bleech. But this is an experiment.
>
> As Glenn says, the review is short enough to do two, three, four reviews, an entire book of reviews, written by me on the same Ripken book, each expressing a different point, or the same point in different language; here wharf foreman, there dancemaster. So where's the beef, huh? What should I look at?
>
> I tried initially to cull the crunchy details from Iron Man and paste them into some A to B form. To Stella and Susan, that worked. But to Michael and Floyd, it didn't. How can I use good details (there are few to spare), and paste it down to a vivid review, giving Michael "something I can't forget"?

To you, this passage probably reads like gibberish, despite the fact that the words I used are, for the most part, conventional, and the sentence structures that house those words, ordinary. From your perspective, this passage might look like a failure of communication. To me, it's just the opposite.

This passage so clearly mirrors the way thoughts bound around my head that even today, fifteen years after I wrote it, I can clearly see all the points I was driving at.

I achieved this miraculous clarity through these three techniques:

1. I used kitchen language.

What's kitchen language? Coined by Ken Macrorie, it's a phrase that describes the language you use around the house when you're lounging in knock-around clothes, as the television hums in the background, and you yap with your best friend on the phone. It's good, strong language, but not the kind you'd normally use to get your point across in most settings. Kitchen language is your own slang, the words you use that best capture the idea of a thought or an object, even if you're the only one who gets what you mean.

In my freewriting excerpt, I used the kitcheny "bleech." What does "bleech" mean?

Judging from the language preceding it—words like "gurgling" and "burp"—I assume that it's a hybrid of "belch" and "retch," and I used it metaphorically, to express the feeling I get when I try to expel ideas during a writing session. "Burp" would have been too weak; "retch" would have been too violent. Therefore, "bleech."

Could I have used more conventional language to make that point to myself? Of course. But during that particular writing session, my racing mind decided "provisional bleech" was what I needed to say.

I didn't sit at my desk and deliberate about it. I merely followed what my mind asked me to write. That's what you should do, too.

Just concentrate on writing loosely and honestly about the subject at hand. Strong kitchen language will come instinctively.

2. I kept quiet about those things that needed no explanation.

Since I was writing for myself, I didn't name all the "characters" involved in the situation or hack through all the background information surrounding it. If I had been writing for others' eyes, of course, I would've had to pencil in some kind of headline, like "Re: My review for the Times." I would've also had to explain that "Glenn" was a publisher friend of mine who'd read an early draft of my review, and so forth and so on. But for myself, it was unnecessary.

3. I jumped around.

When you're writing for other people, you need to develop ideas convincingly and make certain that your readers are clear about where your narrative is headed. In freewriting, however, by following your mind's natural workings, you can drop all pretense to sound argument and logical connections of material. I'm not asking you to delude yourself into accepting faulty arguments. I'm only saying that during any given writing session, your reasoning does not need to be airtight. Feel free to jump around as it suits you.

→ Points to Remember

- Freewriting isn't writing, per se; it's a means of watching yourself think.
- Since you're writing for yourself, you don't need to spit shine

your raw thoughts to please others. All that matters is that you yourself understand your logic, references, word choices, and idiosyncratic ideas.

Try This: What's the best idea or product you've heard about in the last seventy-two hours? Write about it for five minutes, incorporating everything you've learned. (If you like, scribble the secrets at the top of your page as a cheat sheet.)

When your time is up, review your writing. If you can read it aloud and others fully understand it, you're stifling your most honest thinking. Do another five minutes' writing and try to get your exact thoughts on paper.

Chapter 5

Secret #5: Go with the Thought

In the mid-1980s, I took an improvisational theater course, hoping to hone what I considered my most bankable gifts, wit and joke cracking. At the time, I fancied myself something of a Woody Allen in training, and I figured an improv course would give me a wide, well-lit platform for showing off. Boy, was I mistaken.

The teacher of the course was an old-school improv troupe member, and he frowned on his students' attempts to be conspicuously funny on stage. Humor, he preached, must flow naturally from the situation being portrayed and should never be forced into it by Borscht Belt wannabes. So class after class, he would toss a few students on stage, yell out our fictional identities ("Mark, you're a homeless person. Cindy, you're a businesswoman on the way to the train"), and give us a scene to act within ("Mark, you try to convince Cindy to give you money").

Begrudgingly, I delivered lines that logically followed

my partner's lines ("Ma'am, do you have fifty cents for a hot meal?"), while I gulped back the absurdist, out-of-left-field dialogue I longed to deliver ("Ma'am, I just peed on myself"). When that course ended, I turned my back on improv theater ethics, or so I thought.

Half a dozen years later, while freewriting about a troubling business situation, I found myself unexpectedly embracing the improvisational philosophy I had earlier rejected. I wrote:

> Remember your improv training. You must go with the situation set up for you.
>
> If you're taking premise suggestions from the audience and someone wants you to be a dentist giving a cleaning, for example, that's what you must be. You can't suddenly chuck the scenario in mid-speech and say, "Oh, you thought I was a dentist, but I'm really a gynecologist, or a shoe salesman, or a Kodiak bear." Also, you mustn't contradict the lines fed to you from your fellow actors. If a co-player says, "Dr. Levy, here are those X-rays you wanted," you shouldn't say, "I didn't ask for X-rays." That reply kills the scene. There's nothing to say after that.
>
> Instead, if you want the scene to march ahead, you take that X-ray line and create within that context. You pretend to study the X-rays and say something like "Look at this, all your teeth are molars." "Look at this, you have no teeth, only cavities." "Look at this, your teeth aren't numbered like they were in the dental school cadaver." Stuff like that. Be funny if you like, but within the logic presented.

In the few minutes I spent writing this, I realized that the improv ethic—go with what you're given—isn't the cumbersome, rain-soaked woolen overcoat I thought it was. Rather, this philosophy liberates the mind by giving it a specific ground zero to begin thinking. Throughout my subsequent freewriting, I referred to this improv strategy again and again, reminding myself to "go with the thought" I had just put on paper. As my hand raced to keep up with my mind, I felt great energy in my thinking and writing.

Chapter 5   Secret #5: Go With the Thought

The whole time I was scribbling, I would say to myself something like "Go with the thought. Agree with what you just wrote, and logically extend it.... Be whimsical if you like, but make sure the whimsy naturally follows what preceded it.... Based on this new thought that just appeared on the page, what might happen next?"

This intoxicating game of "agreeing and extending," during which I effortlessly fleshed out scenarios, took up pages of my writing until my hand grew tired, my timer went off, or even more important, I had discovered some provisional methods for tackling a problem.

To make this all clearer, let's set up a little learning lab situation for you. Rather than asking you to jump right in and use the concept on a situation from your own life, let's shift the perspective and add some playfulness to your learning.

For the next ten minutes, you're not you. You're Jennifer, a marketer for BeefSalami.com, a year-old company that sells salami over the Internet. Given your well-defined niche, your market share in Web-based salami sales is 90 percent. But your profits aren't where you'd like them to be. What can you do?

To begin (after your "try easy" invocation), you might tell yourself why you're sitting there writing. "Selling salami on the Internet gives us a defined market niche but is far too restrictive to enable us to grow" would do. Then you might ask yourself about the different sides of the business—the product, its marketing, the billing, competitive sites—to see where you'd like to direct your thinking.

Suppose, being a marketer, your attention gravitates toward the public's perception of your product. Most people, you assume, perceive salami as a low-class, sodium nitrite-ridden amalgamation of cow parts stuffed into an edible membrane casing. (You realize, perhaps for the first time, that the cow wasn't born with a specific "salami" organ.) How, you wonder, do we change that perception?

37

What about positioning salami as an upscale product? All right, then, how do you "go with that thought"?

On the paper, you have a starting point—creating an upscale salami—and in your next sentence, you take a step that plays off the thought that preceded it. Perhaps, you write, an upscale salami might be wrapped in gold foil. Good. What else? It might be packaged in a dignified wooden box, like cigars. Snob appeal. Great! An upscale salami might have some kind of medal and ribbon attached, signifying what? Quality meat... an award winner... imported from some romantic locale... sanctioned by some prestigious organization. What organization? The government... an existing industry body... an organization BeefSalami.com helped create?

If I go with that last thought, you wonder, where will it lead me? You have no way of knowing until you write it down and follow its call:

BeefSalami.com could chair some kind of committee to assure the public that Web-based meat products would adhere to high standards, higher, even, than those demanded by the U.S. Government. The U.S. Government? Why stop there? Go with the thought.

BeefSalami.com could chair an industry standards organization that makes certain that Internet meats around the world conform to certain health and taste requirements. Around the world? That would give us an international presence. It's true, you write, that by virtue of being on the Net, BeefSalami.com already has an international presence. But as part of a sanctioning body, the company could form crucial alliances with meat producers from other parts of the globe. We could translate our Web page into two dozen other languages and advertise our product in the appropriate countries as an exotic import.

You continue writing down associative thoughts as they come until you feel you've said what you needed to say. At that point, you stop—or do you? By all means, halt your free-writing if you believe you've ferreted out some good ideas or you have a better handle on your situation. Remember, though, there are other avenues for you to explore if you're up to it.

Despite the seemingly inevitable logic by which each thought grew out of its predecessor, someone else might have taken a particular thought in a different direction. Let's go back to the beginning of our scenario. You've been thinking about the public's perception of salami, but you want to explore an alternate route: Maybe changing the audience's perception of the meat isn't necessary. Maybe BeefSalami.com could play into the fact that the product is a down-and-dirty meat, a meat of the streets. How would you prove that?

Or maybe your initial premise is wrong. Do you know for sure how the public views salami? How might you gather pertinent information about what people think about your luncheon meat, and how might you use this information when you get it?

Is the tight niche of Internet salami seller one your company should continue to work within? Whether it is or not, it's certainly worth a few minutes' time contemplating how you might expand your focus.

And what of the other numerous approaches? So far, you've been looking at the goal of bigger profits through a marketing and sales lens. But how would you approach it from an accounting or operations perspective? You don't need perfect knowledge of these fields to poke around in them, at least in freewriting. A timid first sentence scratched onto the paper and the ability to tease a second timid sentence from that first one will do the trick.

Okay, let's shed our Jennifer persona and reinhabit our own form-fitting personalities. To go with a thought in your own writing, it isn't necessary to choose some vital problem and give it lots of serious, preliminary thought. Just grab a problem, any problem, and write about why it bugs you. Then, as a thought experiment, add a small change to the scene and follow the implications of that change from one scene to the next. If you let your hand move swiftly enough, and you give yourself permission to play, you might just find yourself sporting a fresh idea or two.

→ Points to Remember

- When you go with a thought, you assume that a particular thought is true, and you take a graduated series of logical steps based on the thought. ("If A is true, that means B is true. And if B is true, that means C is true. And if C is true...")
- Since situations are complex structures, there are many directions you can move around in them and still be working within the situation's logic. (For instance, you and I discover that our company's postal meter is broken. If I go with that thought, my logical responses might deal with finding out who's to blame for breaking it; your responses might deal with getting the meter fixed.)

TryThis: What's the worst idea or product you've heard about in the last seventy-two hours? Write about it and go with it for five minutes. At the end of five minutes, reset your timer, and go with it in a completely different direction. Be sure you obey all the secrets of freewriting during this exercise in agreeing and extending.

Chapter 6

Secret #6: Redirect Your Attention

With pen in hand or computer powered up, you begin a free-writing road trip about something important to you. Perhaps you're thinking about how to announce a fee increase, or you're wondering how best to approach your boss to ask for higher-visibility projects. Whatever the situation, you're on the freewriting bus, motoring along, when suddenly you hit the brakes. The road ahead is washed out, and you don't know how to proceed.

Quickly, you consult your checklist of freewriting rules: Try easy, check. Writing fast and continuously, check. Inoffensive kitchen timer counting down ten-minute intervals, check. Now you've run out of ideas. You've reached the end of your thoughts, or so you believe.

While you stare ahead at the washed-out road, a distant light glimmers to your left. Why, there's a highway out there! How could you have missed it? Then, to your right, a loud honk. By gum, a road leading to a major city! Yet you passed it without noticing.

You look around. Roads, exits, and towns are everywhere, only you failed to see them while your eyes were trained ahead. I call these roads, exits, and towns "focus-changers," and they're available to you on every freewriting road trip.

But what exactly is a focus-changer? Nothing more than a question you ask yourself on paper that requires you to comment on something you've just written. It keeps your fingers and mind moving.

Not only do I use focus-changers whenever I write privately, but I use them in public documents, too. As you comb through *Accidental Genius*, you'll constantly see me asking myself questions like:

- What was I thinking here?
- How else can I say that?

Those are two of my favorites. They push me to see again what I've done and think I already know. They also challenge me into generating fresh thought, even after I believe I've run out of road. But those aren't the only focus-changers you can use.

Focus-changers have endless numbers or forms. Here's a partial list of some helpful ones:

- How can I make this exciting?
- How can I add value?
- What else can I say about this subject?
- Why am I stuck at this particular point?
- How can I get unstuck?
- What am I missing here?
- What am I wrong about here?
- Why?
- How can I prove that?
- How can I disprove that?

- What do I think about that?
- If I continue to think that way, what might happen?
- What other problems like this one have I experienced?
- What solutions can I borrow from past problems that can be applied to this current one?
- What does this remind me of?
- What's the best-case scenario?
- What's the worst-case scenario?
- What am I doing right?
- What am I doing brilliantly?
- How can I jump the track?
- Which strengths of mine (or my company's) can I apply?
- Which weaknesses need to be compensated for?
- Where's the proof that that statement is true?
- How am I the wrong person for this project?
- How am I the right person for this project?
- How would an arbitrator judge that?
- If I wanted to make a big mistake here, what would I do?
- What data do I need that I don't yet have?
- How can I better use the data I already have?
- How would I describe the situation to the CEO?
- How would I describe it to my mother?
- How would I describe it to my most supportive friend?
- How would I describe it to a disinterested stranger?

You get the message. When you come face-to-face with a stumper, a puzzler, or bewilderment, use one of these questions to start a new conversation with yourself. Or invent your own.

What you might also do: Reread the list of focus-changers and check off the two or three that most intrigue you. Copy those favored focus-changers onto a scrap of paper and keep it next to you during a freewrite. When you hit a wall, or just for giggles, grab one and see where it leads you.

→ Points to Remember

- Focus-changers are simple questions to ask yourself, in writing, that help you redirect your mind toward the unexplored parts of a situation.

Try This: Reread one of your writing pieces, and note where a focus-changing question would have led you in a different direction. Do ten minutes of freewriting in this new direction. If you start to run dry of ideas before the ten minutes is up, use other focus-changers to revitalize your thinking.

Part Two

Powerful Refinements

If you're trying to solve a problem and logic is failing you, you need to take a more indirect problem-solving approach. Freewriting can help you.

Use the page to adopt wild perspectives and slam together ideas that don't match.

Do those things enough, and you may find that you've fashioned an idea that far outdistances anything you've come up with before.

In this section, you'll read more than a dozen liberating, freestyle, perspective-twisting tools that you can use while freewriting.

Chapter 7

Idea as Product

Writing teachers often tell students that "writing is thinking." They say this to demystify writing and wipe away students' anticipatory tension in putting pen to paper. These reassuring teachers believe that if you can think clearly, and use the language of daily speech, you can express yourself competently on the page.

This is valuable advice. The more we think of writing as nothing special, the more we think of it as just another way of expressing ourselves (like speaking to a friend over the phone), the better off we are.

But for those of us trying to use our writing to solve problems, the logical question is, Why write at all? If "writing is thinking," why not dispense with the writing altogether and get down to some hard thinking? Two reasons, I believe, underline the importance of getting your ideas down on paper, of making them a touchable product.

PART TWO: POWERFUL REFINEMENTS

First, the physical act of moving your pen across the page, or hitting computer keys, is a powerful focusing force.

Human thought, by nature, bounces all over the place; that's why most prolonged bouts of serious thinking degenerate into daydreaming.

Suppose I'm managing some service workers who have a problem communicating with each other in front of customers. These workers normally get into pointless debates about procedure, confuse one another, and end up arguing.

If I try to think my way out of this situation, I may get some strong ideas. But just as likely, my thinking will edge toward tangential affairs until I forget why I initiated my mental problem-solving campaign.

I'll picture the workers in the situation, particularly the troublemaker, Mike. Then I'll remember that Mike owns a Jeep like mine. That'll remind me to take my Jeep to Jiffy Express to get the oil changed. I take it there because the staff shout out the oil-changing actions they take ("Changing the filter!"), and these cries have an impressive, military efficiency to them. I also like the fact that the boss, Russ, knows me and gives me a discount and...

My good problem-solving ideas dissipate, evaporating somewhere between the catalyzing problem and my drive over to Jiffy Express. That, in my experience, is how the human mind works.

There's nothing wrong or unusual about this mental divergence and far-flung association. In this situation, though, I didn't use my mind's natural workings to reach a productive end. That's a trap of thinking without a physical object to focus one's attention.

When you write and create a product as you go, it's a simple matter to bring your attention back to the subject at hand. No swami-like mind control or puritanical discipline is needed. Even as you diverge from your main subject, the fact that you're sitting and scribbling jars you into remembering that you started your writing efforts with a specific purpose.

There's a story about Thomas Edison that relates to this. Edison would hold a handful of coins while resting in his chair, so when he lapsed into sleep, the coins would fall, hit the floor, and wake him—a cacophonous reminder to get back to work.

The physical act of writing is your handful of coins. Let the divergences in your mind come, write about them if you wish, but as your divergence winds down, wake yourself into realizing that you had a starting point that still needs attention.

The second reason you should create a written record of your thinking is that it gives you a path of bread crumbs you can use to retrace your steps. This point is similar to the first one, but with several important distinctions.

In any given bout of freewriting, the drifts your mind takes can hold your richest thinking. It would be a shame if these potentially fertile byways were lost to you because you couldn't recall them. Most people lose the power of these drifts, however, because they trust their memory when they shouldn't.

In one workshop setting, for instance, I informally interviewed students about their jobs for twenty minutes at a time and wrote down key identifying words as they spoke (without letting them see what I was writing), so that I could accurately recall their talks, both main subject and digressions.

I then asked each student to revisit what they said and repeat all the points they could remember. On average, these students remembered only half of what they had told me only moments earlier.

I am asking you, then, to write out your quickly passing thoughts as if they were gold, because some of these thoughts may be of incalculable value to you when examined at the proper time.

If you're pursuing a subject that genuinely interests you, and you write about it in a loose, nonjudging fashion, you never know what answers and creative possibilities the next sentence may hold. To put it another way: If you work with the expectation that your writing will eventually lead you into an area worthy of exploration, you'll find that area.

Look back to the earlier "customer service–Jiffy Express" scenario as an example. I first introduced that anecdote as an example of unproductive daydreaming. My goal was to think up, without committing to paper, a few ideas to solve an important, recurring work problem. But my good intentions drifted off toward getting my Jeep serviced.

If this same digression played out on paper, though, with a chance for me to redirect attention and review some tangential ideas on the page, I might have gotten a possible solution out of the situation.

While writing about Jiffy Express, I might have paid more attention to the military shout-out method their staff uses to service a car. Perhaps such a verbal checklist could be applied to the customer service problem my employees were having? Maybe, maybe not. What's important to note here is how my freewriting acted as a bullpen to hold the digressions in check, so they could be studied for their associative power.

→ Points to Remember

The conversion of your thoughts into a paper product is important because it:

- keeps unproductive daydreaming to a minimum
- allows you to hold your main idea at the forefront of your mind
- permits you to follow your associative line of thinking back to its origin
- gives you something solid to criticize and create from

- enables you to study your thinking from one day to the next

Now you may be thinking, "Wait a minute. This is no recap. Mark didn't overtly discuss all these points in this chapter." That's true. What I did do was reread what I had written, what was staring at me in black and white off the page, and allow the writing to suggest this new point, which I acted on:

- Just as your written product shows you where you've been, it also suggests where you haven't been.

Try This: Write about a problem situation for five minutes, and put it aside. Now, in a second five-minute session, try recalling all the details and digressions you made during the first five minutes. What did you leave out the second time? What did you inadvertently add?

Chapter 8

Prompt Your Thinking

If you've done any freewriting before, you may have heard the term "prompt." A prompt is a type of freewriting exercise. Instead of beginning a session with whatever appears in your mind, you begin with a predetermined phrase (called a prompt) that guides the direction of your writing.

How would using a prompt work? Well, if you were about to loosen up with a ten-minute freewrite and wanted a prompt, I might say, "Complete the following sentence: 'The best part of my workday is.'" That's where you'd begin. You'd answer that question, at least initially. You could stay on it for the entire ten minutes, or you could move to another subject minutes or even seconds after beginning. Your choice.

The number of prompts you could use are endless. Any open-ended phrase will do. You can come up with them on your own. A few more examples:

"Yesterday I saw a curious thing..."

"I'd really impress myself if, starting today, I..."

"If I didn't have to work, I'd..."

"My idea of a boring time is..."

"If I woke to find myself ten feet tall, the first thing I'd do is..."

"I'd like to tell you a story..."

"I threw a stone and it landed..."

"I remember..."

Now, I've used prompts many times, but I've never considered them part of my regular repertoire. Why? It could be arrogance. Maybe I thought that if you've been freewriting as long as I have, you don't need outside direction to guide you. Maybe I grew up watching too many rugged individualist movies, wanted to be my own man, and didn't want outside forces telling me what to do. These are guesses, mind you. I can't be sure why I rarely used prompts.

After speaking with Robyn Steely, though, I have a different view of the technique.

Steely is the executive director of a nonprofit organization, Write around Portland, that works with social service agencies to build community. The organization brings writing workshops to people who might not normally be able to attend because of health, income, and other barriers. It conducts workshops for seniors in foster care, people with mental or physical disabilities, people recovering from addictions, people who have undergone domestic abuse, and the homeless, among others.

The central principle driving Write around Portland's workshops is freewriting.

Participants sit in a circle with pad and pen, and a facilitator begins the session by offering up two prompts, such as "The thing about you and me..." and "The night smelled like...." Each participant chooses one prompt to kindle their writing. Later, they share what they've produced and offer feedback to other writers. In giving feedback, participants keep their comments on the parts of the writing that are strong.

Chapter 8   Prompt Your Thinking

Steely says prompts don't hem in thinking; they open it up. Given the same prompt, one participant might write about what he eats for breakfast while another might write about a wartime battle she fought in.

No matter how big or small the subject matter, the most powerful pieces are, of course, the honest ones. Facilitators, in fact, counsel participants not to overpolish their work or remove truthful facts in favor of ones that seem to sound more professional. When people hear a real detail, they can tell.

Prompts, then, can help people approach material that they may not have thought to write about. They can give a small push in an unexpected direction.

When I asked Steely what makes for a superior prompt, she gave the following advice: "Make your prompts short and open-ended. For instance, 'After the storm...' is a good one. It's only a few words, and it could be about a childhood rainstorm, a thunderstorm, a fight, or it could have nothing to do at all with storms."

Some more examples of prompts you might use:

The two things I could do today to make things more exciting...

I'd love to learn about...

The simplest thing I could do to make a difference would be...

If I did the opposite of everything I normally do, my day would look like this...

I love...

I hate...

I'm scared by...

I have no explanation as to why I haven't done this yet, but I should...

This sounds insane, but my organization would be 500 percent more productive if...

This sounds inconsequential, but...

If I were guaranteed success, the project I'd take on would be...

I'm great at _____, but I'd rather not do it because...

I stink at _____, but I'd like to do it because...

The three things my boss can do to help me are...

The three things I can do to help my boss are...

I need to brush up on...

I should do more...

If I went back to school now, I'd take...

If I didn't have to work, I'd...

I get worried when...

If it were five years into the future, and my entire life were different, I'd be...

The two things I really want to do in my work life, but haven't yet, are...

You know what I'd like to do again?...

The project I'm proudest of is...

I'd really impress myself if, starting today, I...

I should call _____ right away, because...

I know three ways to make a difference in this world, and they are...

If I were giving a commencement speech, I'd tell the students...

When I got in the car...

Here's what I overheard...

When I forgot my wallet...

It was getting dark...

The birds were singing...

I opened the door...

Two days from now...

→ Points to Remember

- Prompts can warm up and send your mind in unanticipated directions.
- The best prompts are short and open-ended.

Try This: Choose one of these two prompts, and do a ten-minute freewrite starting with "I'd like to tell you a story..." or "This sounds inconsequential, but...."

Chapter 9

Open Up Words

Here's a page from my freewriting file:

I yawn when I see an author use the word "empowerment."

Sure, I understand that the word is supposed to mean "decentralization" and "giving everyone, including the front-line worker, power to make decisions that help the customer." But unless the writer is someone I trust, someone I know who has thought about the word 124 times, and put it into practice himself, I think most writers use the word because it sounds high-minded.

The majority of the business world doesn't use empowerment as a practice, at least, not effectively. For most businesspeople, empowerment is an untested concept, or a rationalization for a disinterested, laissez-faire management style.

Here are more problems inherent in the conventional idea of "empowerment." If workers are truly empowered, they're going to make mistakes, probably in front of the customer. Sounds good in a business book, but not so good when a lengthening line of exasperated customers roll their eyes in front of you.... If workers are truly empowered, they may use their autonomy as a way to justify laziness, explaining away their inefficient service as something they thought was necessary, given the situation.

If workers are truly empowered, they still need monitoring because they're executing actions out of the accepting norm, actions that may have untold, companywide ramifications.

I know I'm playing the stinker in this writing. Someone sees what I just wrote and thinks I'm a strict, follow-the-rules, hierarchy guy. Which I'm not. I vehemently believe in empowerment, at times. I do, though, have enough mistrust of people not to hand them the keys to the organizational kingdom just because it seems like the enlightened thing to do.

After eyeing this excerpt, you're probably settling back in your chair and thinking, "Okay, a chapter on the evils of empowerment. How is Levy going to drive home his point, I wonder?" But no, I've pretty much said all I have to say about empowerment, at least in this book. The subject of my excerpt takes a back seat to the method I had in mind while I was generating it. This freewriting excerpt was produced while I engaged in a technique I call "open up words."

When you "open up a word," you redefine that word (or the phrase that contains it) so it has personal meaning. In a sense, you become an explorer within the word, forsaking the sleepy meaning others have given it, and discover for yourself if the concepts embedded within it are still valid. Like a medical student who learns to heal by dissecting a cadaver from head to toe, you strip off the word's skin and unravel its guts to study its fundamental premises. Here's how I go about it:

1. Pick a word to examine.

As you comb through a management text, a magazine article, or your freewriting, or as you work your way through a business day, you'll come across words whose definitions seem taken for granted, words that are used as a way to stop thinking rather than start it. These are the words to pay attention to.

Perhaps you'll happen upon a term like "empowerment," which people uncritically accept as goodness incarnate. That's a word to set aside for study. Perhaps you'll discover a term like "budget cut," which instantly brings on sour stomach. Words in this camp also deserve a closer look.

Perhaps, too, you'll run into a term like "industry," whose meaning seems neutral. These words often yield the grandest surprises when deconstructed through your writing.

2. Give yourself a common definition of the word.

If you look back to my empowerment excerpt, you'll see that I begin by laying bare the word for what it really is, including its most overused, lifeless connotations. I tell myself what other people "see" when they discover the word on a page or come upon it in life.

3. Ask yourself if you agree, or disagree, with the common definition, and explain your choice.

Because you've already put down a base definition on the page, you have written thoughts to build upon.

4. Ask yourself what kind of thoughts and images you may have the next time you come across the word.

After slogging through people's dead language, playing with your own insights, and arguing up a storm, your equilibrium may be thrown off if you don't summarize where you've been and what you've learned. Tell yourself, in a simple paragraph or two, how you've strengthened your "knowing" through opening up the word.

Let's put all I've mentioned together and see how "open up words" operates in practice.

From my bookshelves, I've drawn a volume, *Expanding Our Now* by Harrison Owen, in which I'd previously underlined this paragraph:

> Management would have you believe that there is a procedure for every necessary activity, and of course work must be done according to the procedure. But the reality is rather different. More than occasionally it is necessary to "work around" the procedures to get something done. Work-arounds are treated as exceptions, but I strongly suspect work-arounds are the rule.

Certainly, these sentences are without fog or an ounce of obscurifying fat. But without opening up that word "work-arounds," we may forget the concept by the time our eyes have skipped to the next paragraph. Here's how you might give that phrase a deeper reading through freewriting:

> "Work-around" is Owen's expression for doing things not-by-the-book, in order to get results. That phrase sounds right to me, but why?
>
> For the most part, I believe we perform certain tasks today because people before us performed those tasks. If different people preceded us, we'd today perform different tasks.
>
> It's kinda like a "What would have happened if…" speculation story, where, say, the Nazis won World War II. If they had won, I probably wouldn't be sitting here typing on my laptop about this subject. Instead, I may never have existed. Or I'd have existed and died. Or I'd be doing something perhaps far removed from what I'm doing now.
>
> Same thing with regards to the goals we value and the way we go about obtaining those goals.

Chapter 9 Open Up Words

I value literature, but that's because there was a literature system in place when I arrived in this life. If the people before me hadn't valued literature so highly and, instead, found great personal expression in, say, collecting leaves, maybe my goal today would be leaf collection. I don't think I'm that creative or iconoclastic that I would have pioneered the field of literature by myself. I wouldn't have thought about the written word, and if I did, I probably would have thought it trivial.

This idea of those-before-us-set-ground-work-for-the-way-we-operate-today holds in smaller ways, too.

When my lawn is overgrown, I either fire up the mower or call a service. But I do those things because I was taught to do them, overtly or through a kind of lawn care osmosis. If the hordes of people before me hadn't thought that tending to lawns was important, I'm sure I wouldn't be doing it today. If those pre-me people never had lawns, I'm pretty certain I'd never have one. Okay, Levy, ground yourself. How does all this talk of Nazis and lawn care relate to the phrase "work-arounds"?

This way: "work-around" sounds like when you do it, you're doing something wrong. It sounds like, "Sure you're getting the job done, but you're being unnecessarily show-offy and difficult in order to do it—a cheater, not a team player." Actually, though, when you (appropriately) "work-around," you show that you understand that most processes are jerry-rigged—that is, there's nothing sacred about them; they're just there to accomplish a goal. If other unused, or unthought-of, processes help you get the job done better, then use those.

How have I worked-around? I remember the time I helped a bookstore client of mine get books for their author signing.

A prominent author was coming that night to do an announced signing, and the store discovered they didn't have enough copies of the author's book for her to autograph.

Now my involvement should have conventionally stopped when I told the store's book buyer that I couldn't get him copies in time for the event. But I worked-around this standard answer with some divergent thinking, and by overstepping what would normally be considered my boundaries.

I gave the buyer a bunch of options that he'd never heard of before but seemed reasonable to me: Call the author and see if she has stock she'd bring; call her publisher and see if they could jet over stock; if the normal channels at the publisher were stock-poor, make sure to check with the author's editor, who might have sample copies around; ask to borrow copies from friendly, surrounding stores; buy copies from rival surrounding stores to save face (I'd place the calls, if he liked); offer to ship the book for free, and affix an autographed sticker inside it, when the stock did arrive.

Through a combination of these strategies, everyone came away from the signing happy. This story may not have the power of my Nazi victory scenario, but it works for me. I demonstrated this concept of work-around by using every unconventional method I could think of to get my customer books, even if my involvement overstepped what a wholesaler rep should do.

So with all I've just written, what should I take away with me about "work-around"? If you truly want a result, don't worship the conventional route that most people follow. That route was probably invented through trial and error, and if different trials and errors had been attempted, you'd have a different route to take today.

Before we finish here, note this intriguing point: I began the chapter by opening up "empowerment" and finding the concept lacking. I finished the chapter, however, by opening up "work-around" and finding it invigorating. What are the similarities and differences between the two? Perhaps you'd like to write about it.

→ Points to Remember

- To open up a word, write down four things: a word for study, the generally agreed-upon definition of that word, your thoughts on the accuracy of the definition, and a personal definition that suits your eccentric tastes.

- In freewriting, always explain to yourself why you think what you think. Often, you'll realize you have no basis for your belief. What then? Apply a little mental elbow grease, and come up with a belief that will better serve you.

Try This: Make a list of five common jargon words in your industry, and open up each for five minutes.

Chapter 10

Escape Your Own Intelligence

The day's workshops had ended at the business writers' conference, and I was relaxing in the dining room with the other attendees. A woman at a table in the corner caught my attention. She was drawing with a fat marker on the butcher paper tablecloth. I headed over.

The paper was black with scribbles. There were circles, triangles, and half-completed equations. Arrows pointed every which way. The whole thing looked dauntingly elaborate, like she was planning a moon shot.

I asked her what she was creating, and her answer was not what I expected. She told me she was diagramming a way people could converse more clearly and directly.

The woman said she was a business school professor, came to the conference because she wanted to write a book, and figured the communications model she was working on could be the basis for one. Creating it was slow going. She couldn't make it click.

She began explaining the model. It was so abstract that it was hard to tell it involved human beings at all. She wasn't developing it from life. She was creating it by heaping theory on top of theory. In trying to complete it, she was running into conceptual walls.

After talking about the model and its difficulties for twenty minutes, she wondered what I thought. Now I'm like a vampire. I only come in when I'm invited. She invited me in. "Remember, what you've drawn isn't reality," I said, tapping the butcher paper. "It's a problem-solving model in service of you. It's a tool that's supposed to make things easier. If it's not working, simplify it or throw it out. If it's making you stuck, it's a bad model."

The woman wasn't happy, but she understood. She was pushing to make her model work because she assumed that to get published she needed a concept that was big and sophisticated. Lots of moving parts. But you don't often make ideas better by complicating them.

At times we fall prey to our own smarts. We trap ourselves with notions that sound good but don't work in practice. So how do you escape your own intelligence?

I follow the advice of Ken Macrorie. Rather than "trying to be lucky with a Great Idea," he said, "reach for a fact."

Coming up with facts is easy. There's no strain, no indecision. You can spit them out like seeds. Facts ground you by moving your attention from your tangled thoughts to the tangible world. Amassing facts often gets you to see solutions that had previously been invisible.

While freewriting, which facts should you reach for? Obvious ones. Ones right in front of you.

Let's say you run a small accounting firm, you want to start an e-newsletter, and you're biting your nails over it.

What should the newsletter be about? Who's its best audience? Who'll do the writing? How should it be distributed? How will you manage it while doing your other work?

You decide to write about the situation. Where do you begin? The obvious:

> I want to create an e-newsletter, and I'm not sure how. Let's start with some obvious things.

> My company does accounting for small businesses grossing $500,000 to $5 million. Mostly service businesses. We get them through word of mouth. What else is obvious?

> For a numbers guy, I can write. But I write slow. Used to take me ten straight hours to write a column for the school paper. Had ten hours to spare because I was a student and had days off. That gives me an idea.

> In a hundred-mile radius we have four colleges. Maybe I can find students from those schools to do the writing? Heck, maybe I can find students from other parts of the country to do the writing? Who would I call to find out? The person at each school in charge of internships or work programs, I guess. OK, so I have one to-do item: Contact colleges for students who know something about accounting and who can write.

> Back to what's obvious. I subscribe to seven or eight newsletters. How do those companies distribute their material? I think each lists its distribution service at the bottom of the newsletter. Never thought of that before. So, I'll check on that.

> What else? I never get any of those newsletters at the end of the week. They always come in the beginning of the week: Monday or Tuesday, I believe. I should check. So there might be some data on when it's best to send a newsletter.

Listing obvious facts has a calming effect that unclenches the mind. One fact leads to another, which leads to another, on down the line.

You're under no obligation to make your list of facts follow some logical order. There's no A through Z here. You're still freewriting, and you should approach your obvious-fact writing with the same abandon and energy you use during any bout of writing. Jump around as much as you'd like. Leave a fact as soon as you find one more intriguing.

→ Points to Remember

- At times our minds add uncalled-for complexity to situations.
- If you've thought yourself into a corner and are stuck, free-write about the situation by listing everything in it that's obvious. Put down simple facts. They have a way of cutting through the fog.

Try This: Call to mind a problem that's bugged you lately, a problem with seemingly no solution. Freewrite for ten minutes about what's obvious in it. Simple facts. Facts about the situation, what you think, what others think, what has been tried, what you could try, what's holding things back, what's rational, and what's irrational. Don't create a linear list. Let one fact suggest the next. See if this approach creates any openings in the problem.

Chapter 11

The Value in Disconnecting

When I speak to groups, I have them freewrite at their seats. I ask questions like "How could you quadruple your productivity in a week?" and "What things would you like to do but haven't yet done in life?" They answer with pad and pen, and we discuss their responses.

For most of the day, I keep the writing periods short, five to fifteen minutes. Near day's end, though, I ask them to go all out and write for thirty minutes nonstop. Believe me, my request sends a charge through the audience.

They realize that no one, except maybe a mystic, writes for thirty minutes straight, and the thing you haven't done is almost always worth doing (at least if it's not dangerous). Who knows what will happen? Hand cramps? Nausea? Visions? Shape-shifting? The only way to find out is by trying.

At the very least, the participants return home with a story. Writing continuously for that long may not rank up there with running a marathon or climbing a mountain, but it's noteworthy.

Anyway, while they're writing, be it for five minutes, thirty minutes, or something in between, I walk throughout the audience to check on how they're doing. I offer encouragement and crack jokes.

I never read what they're writing. Nonetheless, I can tell the exact moment when the writing for them starts to click. As I walk by, I jab my finger down on the page and say, "Here's where you started saying something important" and "Here's where your thinking came alive."

Almost always, the participants agree. They wonder how I could know.

My trick has a simple explanation: When they begin, participants tend to write in a cramped script that fits on the line neatly. Once they loosen up, once they tire, once their internal editor starts to recede and they viscerally connect with the material, their handwriting relaxes.

It happens all of a sudden, and it's easy to spot, even if they're facing me and all I can see is their pads upside down. Their letters grow large and loopy, and they take up several lines. Their words grow fainter, because they stopped pressing on the paper so hard.

It's an unclenching of hand and brain. It's the point where they stopped worrying about being correct and polite and began using the part of their mind that's original and raw.

Afterwards, I conduct a little research. I ask participants what caused the click. The responses vary.

One group tells me that things started clicking when they got tired. It's as if they were using all this energy to keep their normal way of thinking in place, but once that became too much effort, they dropped the pose, and more candid writing began to flow.

A second group tells me that it happened while they were following a thought. They were writing about something meaningful to them, and by exploring all the ways of looking at that thought, by testing its limits, they forgot themselves and got caught up in the writing.

A third group, however, tells me something different. Being tired or fresh didn't enter into it. Nor were they following a thought. In fact, they were doing the opposite of following a thought. The thing that triggered a click with the material was when they disengaged with the thought they had been playing with and followed a new and truer thought.

They disconnected from what wasn't working and used it to catapult them into a better direction.

Pat Schneider wrote that "disconnections are as important as connections. One image triggers another, and like a person walking on large rocks across a creek where the water is fast and slippery, we will not get to the fifth rock that allows us to step onto the opposite bank unless we first step on, and then abandon, rocks number one, two, three, and four."

It's important, then, not to stay with a thought out of duty. Don't think, for instance, that you've invested time and effort thinking about a particular solution and that you must, for some reason, stay with it. One thought leads to the next, which leads to the next. Some thoughts are like stages in a rocket. They get you in the air, but they're going to have to drop off if you're to make it into space. Think of any thought as useful but expendable.

When I abandon a thought, I'm none too delicate about it. It might include some bile:

> So the way to bring in more business is by running a white paper series. Whoa! A white paper series? I can't even feign excitement. It's not for me. Instead, I'm going to start thinking about ramping up my speaking gigs. What would that look like?

Other times I don't care enough about an idea to finish the thought or comment on it. A few taps of the space bar, and I'm on to something else:

PART TWO: POWERFUL REFINEMENTS

Right now, my business is all about creating strategy. Maybe I should include a few execution options like writing plans
I remember the other day when I was speaking with Jake and we were discussing…

Still other times, I'll disconnect from a thought, but before I go rushing to the next idea, I'll think about what I've learned:

Enough with thinking about doing a podcasting campaign. I'm going to explore other strategies. What I am taking away from the podcasting campaign, though, is that I need to have a way of regularly reaching people, and people need a reason to visit me regularly.

Writing about disconnections reminds me of one of my favorite essays, "Writing Off Subject," by Richard Hugo. In it, Hugo talks about teaching students how to write poems. His advice, however, can be applied to ideation and freewriting. Hugo writes:

The poet puts down the title: "Autumn Rain." He finds two or three good lines about Autumn Rain. Then things start to break down. He cannot find anything more to say about Autumn Rain, so he starts making up things, he strains, he goes abstract, he starts telling us the meaning of what he has already said. The mistake he is making, of course, is that he feels obligated to go on talking about Autumn Rain, because that, he feels, is the subject. Well, it isn't the subject. You don't know what the subject is, and the moment you run out of things to say about Autumn Rain start talking about something else.

When you freewrite, the page is alive. The ideas that appear on it will change radically, if you let them. You must be open to the truth of the material as it shows up. When something good materializes, jump on it, whether it fits what you've been writing or not. Don't be afraid to turn your back on what got you there.

→ Points to Remember

- In exploratory writing, your disconnections are as important as your connections. Think of every thought and image as a stepping-stone that might lead you to the idea you need most.
- How you disconnect is up to you. You can trash a thought, turn your back on it, or derive lessons from it. No one way is better than the others.

Chapter 12

Using Assumptions to Get Unstuck

A few years back, my wife asked for help in designing a magic trick. Now, asking me to design a trick isn't such an odd request, given that I've been interested in magic for forty years and have written books on the subject. This request, though, had a catch.

My wife needed the trick, not for entertainment purposes, but for use in a computer course. It seems she was learning an advanced computer language, and her professor gave the class an assignment that sounded a lot like a mind-reading stunt.

The assignment went like this: Design a program that reveals, in ten guesses or less, a number from 1 to 99, secretly chosen by the computer.

I grabbed a pad and pen, and went to work.

"Tell the computer to secretly select a number," I said while scribbling, "and then ask it: 'Did you select a single-digit number?' If the computer says yes, name single-digit numbers until you hit the correct one. If it says no, eliminate single-digit numbers from your search. Next, ask the computer if it chose an even number. If it says yes, eliminate odd numbers from your search. If it says no..."

In short order, I had the trick worked out and could finger any selected number in ten guesses, tops. It was not an entertaining or deceptive trick, but nonetheless, it fit the bill. My wife studied my notes.

"Excellent!" she said, "Now all I have to do is take this mathematical algorithm you wrote and..."

"Wait a minute," I said. "Mathematical algorithm? That I wrote? What do you mean?"

My wife explained that all the steps that went into the creation of the trick could be rightfully tagged "mathematical algorithm." In fact, she complimented me on my mathematical mind.

"Mathematical mind? I regularly failed math in school," I said.

Here I was, the trick's inventor, and I had been the one it fooled. I was thinking tricks, but I was doing mathematical algorithms.

My question to you, then, is this: Where in life might you be better served by thinking "tricks," rather than "algorithms"? Or put another way: How can you recast what you already know to help you understand what you don't?

Remember, this is more than an exercise in semantics; it's a perspective-twister that has critical implications for how you approach a problem.

In my own example, had my wife asked me to write her an algorithm, I, quite literally, wouldn't have known step one about how to do it. I'd have been embarrassed, my wife would have been disappointed, and I would have missed the satisfaction of doing a task I enjoy.

This idea of substituting concepts to solve problems isn't

new. Substituting concepts is one of the ways you go about creating paradigm shifts.

A paradigm is a situation-dependent assumption or set of assumptions that helps us solve problems. Unfortunately, the assumptions that assist us can blind us to other ways of acting.

Seventeen hundred years ago, people believed the earth was flat. In a way, that paradigm, that assumption, helped them because it gave them rules on living and staying safe. They didn't travel far because... they knew they'd fall off the earth. They didn't do business far away because... they knew they'd fall off the earth. They didn't sail far because... they knew they'd fall off the earth. Their assumption may have been constraining, but it kept their world in order. It hurt and helped them.

Today, the flat earth paradigm seems quaint. But we, too, have paradigms operating in all parts of our lives that unnecessarily lock us into ways of thinking and behaving. How do you expose and bust out of those paradigms? The same way I wrote that algorithm: You unintentionally or intentionally ignore the rules of the situation and substitute new ones.

In the story that opened this chapter, I created movement in the situation by substituting a familiar concept ("tricks") for a foreign one ("algorithms"). But you can just as easily shake things up by doing the opposite and substituting a foreign concept for a familiar one. Let's look at how that works.

A few years ago, when I cowrote a book on persuasion, a sports reporter phoned and asked me to comment on a story. He told me a Major League Baseball team had traded their two best players for a bunch of no-name rookies. It was a fire-sale strategy the team's owners used year after year. Why do it?

The reporter claimed that the owners didn't want to pay the stars the tens of millions of dollars each would command in salary. Instead, the owners could now pay the untested rookies a few hundred thousand dollars apiece. From that angle, it saved ownership an enormous sum.

The trouble, though, had to do with season ticket sales. When it came to season tickets, the team had long had among the worst sales in baseball. Many analysts pointed to the owners' proclivity to trade away its stars for cheaper talent. Each year, the fans felt betrayed and expressed their ire by holding back on ticket purchases.

The reporter wondered how I, a persuasion guy, would persuade disgruntled fans to buy season tickets to watch a group of unknowns. What advice would I give the team's owners?

The first thing that hit me was paradigms and assumptions. Judging from the perennially low attendance figures, the team's owners had some odd assumptions about building a fan base. Or perhaps they were just blind to the options in front of them. A way of busting through their blinders was through concept substitution.

"If the problem is how to build a ticket-buying fan base for a group of unknowns," I told the reporter, "the thing the owners should do is see who else has solved that problem. In other words, who has built the biggest, most rabid fan base from nothing, and how did they go about building it?"

The first place I suggested that the owners look at is other Major League Baseball franchises. Maybe they'd spot a tactic that looked interesting. More than likely, though, they'd see fan-base-building strategies that were familiar to them, since they were in the same business and probably operated from similar assumptions.

The next place they could look at is franchises in other professional North American sports, such as the National Football League, the National Basketball Association, and the National Hockey League. They'd have comparable fan-base-building practices to baseball, but their situations were different enough so they wouldn't be identical.

After looking there, I'd advise the team's owners to look at sports in other countries to understand how they solved the problem. Baseball was invented in America, but it has die-hard fans in Japan. How did that happen? What can be learned from there and applied here?

Where the baseball team's ownership would really learn something new, though, was outside the world of sports. How were fan bases built for ideas and initiatives in other fields, such as politics, music, philosophy, medicine, manufacturing, engineering, urban planning, reality TV, and community activism?

Looking into other fields was where the real paradigm shift can occur. The reason: Every field has perceptual blinders, but one field's blinders are probably different from the next field's. When you look through their lens, you see things in an entirely fresh way.

The reporter knew politics. He said that creating a fan base for an unknown reminded him of the Democrats and John Kerry. When Kerry was nominated for president in the primary, he was not well known across the country. The Democrats had to come up with ways of getting him fans in a hurry.

The reporter began mentioning the Democrats' strategies. Each time he did, we applied it to the baseball team's situation. Some of our ideas seemed silly. Some seemed mundane. But some seemed unusual and practical. We laughed at how good some of these ideas were, when just moments earlier we had nothing.

How then would you use concept substitution in your freewriting? Use the page to ask and answer these four questions:

1. What problem am I trying to solve?

   (Be general in your wording here. Nothing too specific. Examples of good general problem statements: "How do I build a fan base for something unknown?" "How do I sell a product to a market that thinks it understands the product when it doesn't?" "How do I reduce costs while increasing coverage?")

2. Who has solved it?
3. How have they solved it?
4. How can I apply their solution to my problem?

Unlike most of the strategies in this book, you're likely to have to do some light research to make concept substitution work. After all, you want to get an idea about how fields that have nothing to do with yours have solved your type of problem. You can't know that off the top of your head. Once you've done some reading, you can use your freewriting to noodle on all the ways of applying it.

→ Points to Remember

- Assumptions help us lead productive lives. At times, though, formerly helpful assumptions can hinder us when we don't realize they're there or we misapply them.
- How can we check for our assumptions? By using freewriting to play with a situation's rules.
- There are two ways to play with the rules: (1) Pretend an unfamiliar part of the problem is familiar, and (2) pretend a familiar part of the problem is unfamiliar. Follow the consequences of each, and see if playing with them creates movement in the situation.

Try This: Think of a problem that's stumped you, and freewrite for ten minutes about people who have solved a similar problem. Consider problem solvers in your field and those far afield. What might happen if you applied some of their strategies to your situation?

Chapter 13

Getting a Hundred Ideas Is Easier Than Getting One

Ready for a piece of lifesaving advice? When you have to come up with an idea, don't try coming up with just one. That'll kill you. I can think of four broad reasons why:

1. When looking for a single idea, we often demand perfection from that idea. What happens? We study any notion through a microscope, magnify its flaws, and dissect its weaknesses. Few candidates can survive such probing.

2. Worse yet, our critical search depresses us and weakens our powers of ideation, because we start expecting everything we dream up to be defective.

3. Then there are times we're so desperate for a home run idea that our standards drop. We'll latch on to any notion that appears. This happens during brainstorming meetings. The busy participants wait until the last minute to hold the meeting, they blow half of it getting up to speed on the topic to be discussed, and then they feel pressured. The first halfway decent thought becomes, by default, "the big idea." The entire brainstorm tilts toward that idea. All the satellite ideas people

create are in support of that dominant one. Now the partici-pants have no choice. They've wasted time, put all their effort into that initial idea, and now must use it despite its merits or problems.

4. Finally, there are times when we grab the first idea because, face it, we're feeling lazy. By coming up with one idea, we can stop thinking so hard and go back to more automatic, knee-jerk, sleepwalking thoughts.

If searching for a single idea is a bad strategy, what's bet-ter? Try searching for a hundred ideas. Finding a mountain of ideas is easier, far easier, than finding one. How is that possible?

Think of the two approaches as games: "the best idea game" and "the lots of ideas game." The goals and strategies of each are completely different. One is grandmaster chess, and the other is 52 pickup.

Goals

The goal of the "best idea game" is to find a high-quality idea. The goal of the "lots of ideas game" is to amass ideas. There's a big difference, right?

Strategies

In the "best idea game," you have to create and judge simul-taneously. It's like using the gas pedal and the brake pedal in traffic. In the "lots of ideas game," your concerns about good and bad are meaningless. You're looking for volume. It's like picking apples. You don't taste each one as you pick it. You just drop it in a basket, with no judgments and no slowing down.

Obviously, there's less effort in playing and winning the "lots of ideas game." But how can it possibly work better when you really do need a killer idea? Simple.

Chapter 13 Getting a Hundred Ideas Is Easier Than Getting One

You can't create a killer idea from thin air. You've got to have material to work with. You need an inventory of thoughts to draw from. If you don't write things down, if you're slow in writing them down, or if you try judging their worth too soon, you won't have anything to create with, just thin air.

You've got to treat each thought as if it's as good as the next. Each thought might be an answer, or it might be a link to an answer. As William Stafford wrote, good or bad, one thought "will help the next thing come."

To play the "lots of ideas" game, let's look at what I mean by an "idea."

Suppose you run an antique furniture store and are looking for greater visibility. You decide to start a blog. Congratulations. Starting a blog counts as an idea. It's that simple. The threshold is that low.

What might your blog be about?

Idea: It could be about the inventory in your store.

Idea: It could be about antique furniture without overtly referencing your store.

Idea: It could be about eighteenth-century furniture, a specialty of yours.

Idea: It could be about nineteenth-century furniture, another specialty of yours.

Idea: It could incorporate both your specialties and be about pre-twentieth-century furniture.

Idea: It could be about antique furniture collectors' lifestyle, which means you could write about furniture, art, wine, entertaining, travel, and the like.

Idea: It could be about lifestyle, and you could post about a specific topic on set days of the week, such as "Art Monday" and "Wine Friday."

We could continue for hours, but you see what I mean. Getting ideas isn't hard. Your idea threshold should be low, because one idea leads to the next. You want to think about abundance.

In a writing session, don't ask yourself, "What's the best idea I can dream up?" Ask yourself, "What are all the ideas I can dream up?"

If you're looking to solve a problem, don't ask, "What's the solution here?" Ask, "In what ways might I solve this problem?"

One person who understood the abundance approach was Donald Murray, the late writing coach for the *Boston Globe*. Murray would counsel reporters to write not one or two lead paragraphs. He'd suggest they write fifty to seventy-five leads before committing to one. And remember, these were reporters on deadlines.

To write fifty or seventy-five leads, they'd have to write fast and loose, trying different angles. One angle might open with a quote. Another might feature a startling statistic. Another might move in close on a single story detail. Another might be an exchange between two people in the story. And so on.

The reporters would take a couple of hours to write these out, look them over, and decide which to use. They'd continue writing the story from there.

Rather than wasting time, this approach saved time since, once they started writing, the reporters knew they had picked the best idea from the many.

→ Points to Remember

- When you need an idea, don't try for just one. When searching for one great idea, we demand perfection from it, depress ourselves, become desperate, and end up latching on to subpar notions.
- Go for lots of ideas. Keep your threshold low. One idea leads to the next—if you let it.

Try This: Over the next two days, use your freewriting to come up with a hundred possible solutions for one of your dearest problems. That's right, 100. Some of the solutions can be mundane, others can be outrageous, and still others can be silly.

Chapter 14

Learn to Love Lying

If you're like me, learning the next technique will be difficult. It goes against what we were taught as children and how we've lived our lives. The technique is lying.

You're going to have to learn to lie. I'll explain.

One of the things that hinders problem solving is that problem situations can seem liked closed environments. The players, beliefs, conflicts, history, and goals appear to be set in stone, with no options.

Such rigidity, however, is usually an illusion. People, situations, and beliefs change. Bigger systems surround and interact with the system you're operating in. There can be lots of room for movement.

If you free yourself from the perceived rigidity of the situation and see things from enough perspectives, you can almost always find usable solutions.

One way of seeing a seemingly fixed situation differently is to tell a lie about it.

Who are you lying to? Yourself. While freewriting, you're playing a trick on yourself so you can escape the claustrophobia of the situation and widen your view. A single falsehood can cause a chain reaction of consequences that can be useful in causing movement in your thinking.

Suppose you're a computer consultant, and you're having a tough time prospecting for clients while servicing your current ones. During the course of three nights of writing, you've dumped a lot of facts and opinions into your freewriting file. You feel as if you have a clear understanding of the situation, but you're no closer to a solution.

A particular aspect feels important to you, though: Your current clients love the fact that you give them extra work for free during the course of a project. They look at your unbilled hours as their much-deserved "value-added extra" for hiring you.

This is the spot in your writing where you try a capricious reality-tweaking experiment. It's time to lie.

Instead of giving your clients these extra hours for free, you are now going to charge for them, and not just charge any rate. A jumbo rate. Two, three, four, even a thousand times your normal fee.

One thousand times your normal fee: You like the way that sounds.

Now go with that lie. Based on this mammoth fantasy fee, how would everything in the situation change, particularly as it relates to your prospecting efforts?

For one thing, your clients would value your normal hours more than they usually do. Since overtime might cost them hundreds of thousands of dollars, they'd have all their supporting work done and waiting for your expertise, because they wouldn't want you to hit "golden time." And since you wouldn't be putting in extra time, you'd have your nights free to plan and execute your marketing campaign.

Of course, if you did reach overtime, you'd make so much money that you could afford to let your prospecting lapse, at least for a while.

What else might happen because of your exorbitant charges?

Companies would think of your service as more valuable to them in order to justify their expenditure on you.

They'd pay you a generous retainer's fee, so you wouldn't bring your brilliance to their competitors.

The major financial magazines and television shows would pick up on your story and do profiles on your monetary wizardry. You wouldn't, at that point, need to prospect since you'd be turning away thousands of multinationals demanding your service.

You could lower your normal hourly rate, since your overtime rate and retainer turned you into a tycoon.

Or you could take the opposite approach: Raise your normal rate and lower your overtime. Or you could lower both your rates, and save on taxes. Or you could become classified as a national treasure. Or you could ask for payment in plutonium...

While you investigated these ridiculous, yet intriguing scenarios, you'd no doubt be smiling and unclogging some pathways in your mind that had been blocked from slavishly following reality's constraints.

Sure, in one sense, this kind of writing seems to be a time-waster, because these fantastic scenarios probably won't happen. But in another, very real sense, you'd be gaining time; you'd be quickly creating the raw material that your more practical side could cobble into a doable solution.

If an element in your situation is:

- small, think of it as tiny or jumbo
- tall, think of it as sixty stories high or the subbasement
- red, think of it as black or paisley
- time-sensitive, think of it as overdue or needs to be finished in fifty years

- important, think of it as critical or trite
- thin, think of it as withered or obese
- clever, think of it as genius or dopey
- velvet, think of it as rose petals or canvas
- an expense, think of it as an investment or a step toward bankruptcy
- loud, think of it as an air horn blast or a whisper
- a nuisance, think of it as intolerable or a blessing
- abnormal, think of it as freakish or natural
- crowded, think of it as bulging or empty
- funny, think of it as side-splitting or grave
- wet, think of it as soggy or tumbleweed dry

Remember, you can always work your way back to reality from your lie. Without consciously playing with fantasy created from a lie, however, you may never realize the potential that awaits you.

→ Points to Remember

- Under the guise of being "realistic," we often limit ourselves more than we need to. One way out of this trap is to consciously use lying in our freewriting as a way of testing alternate universes and ways of acting.
- When you play the lying game, you pick out an arbitrary spot in a situation to go with until all realism falls apart. Later, you can sift through what you've scribbled for flecks of valuable thought.

Try This: Pick an interesting observation you've made in the past two weeks, and write about it for ten minutes, paying particular attention to its most curious feature. In the course of your writing, go with this feature, making it more pronounced, and examine how the rest of your observation changes because of your lie.

Chapter 15

Hold a Paper Conversation

Me: My problem, lately, is that when I meet with resistance from a sales prospect, I get taken aback. See, I've done this job for so many years, and have made my accounts so much money, that I assume everyone should trust me implicitly and instantly see the enormous value in dealing with me. I know that's the wrong way to feel, but it happens.

David: Actually, there are at least two reasons why there's nothing wrong with feeling that way. First, as you know through experience, feelings just happen—sometimes for no traceable reason—so it's unnecessary to hold yourself responsible for having a specific feeling. Second, if you really have helped many customers over the years, then these prospects probably would benefit in dealing with you—only they might not be aware of that.

The only problem I see would be if you let your feelings adversely affect your behavior when dealing with these prospects. If you, for instance, speak harshly to them or don't follow through on what you say you'll do.

Me: Right. That's a good way of looking at it.

David: A realistic way, yes.

Me: Let me see if I understand this: As long as I want new accounts, I'm going to meet people who don't know me or my reputation. My job, then, is to accept my feelings as they are and try to educate them—through word and deed—why they should deal with me.

David: Yes.

Now, that conversation with David Reynolds—a prominent practitioner of Zen-based, Japanese therapies—helped me immeasurably. In it, David reminded me to do what was under my power to control and leave the uncontrollable alone. But there's something else you should know about that conversation: It never happened.

David, to be sure, does exist, and I've had a dozen enlightening conversations with him, but this one I made up during a freewriting session. I had a workplace problem that needed a little study, and I thought my paper version of David could help me examine it in a productive way. I could have just as easily summoned up Steve Jobs, Susan B. Anthony, or my local grocer, and I would have received different counsel. The choice was mine to make and easy to carry out, given the freedom of the freewriting page. Having conversations with others in your writing is most certainly a make-believe game. After all, I couldn't know for certain how David Reynolds would answer me, unless I actually spoke with him, but it's a perspective- and indirection-powered game that offers the freewriter genuine benefits.

Here's one example: Lynn Kearney, a business writing consultant, told me about an executive she was coaching who used imaginary dialogues in his writing to dramatically boost company salaries.

The executive, she said, held several weeks of make-believe conversations in a notebook so he'd be able to go before a board of directors—including Alan Greenspan—and make a case for pay increases. By the time the actual meeting came about, he had answers for every objection the board raised. He went into the situation confident and came out with hefty bonuses for his employees.

So, holding a paper conversation can help you rehearse how you'd handle a tough situation, lock in knowledge you already have, and explore a topic with someone who has already been there.

Holding a paper conversation also gives you the advantages of speaking with a good bartender: You feel listened to, and you learn things about yourself and your situation, even though the bartender's only contribution to the talk is putting coasters and napkins in front of you.

Who should you speak with? Dialoguing with a variety of people, in a host of far-out ways, makes for a paradigm-smashing experience:

- Hold a paper conversation with a coworker who's giving you problems because he's acting like a jerk. Find out why he's acting like a jerk.
- Converse with a coworker who has successfully handled a project you're currently tackling. Discover how she did it.
- Discuss a dear topic with someone who holds a view wildly different from your own. Try understanding his position, add to it, and then knock it down.
- Speak to a fictional person who has a combination of thoughts and behaviors drawn from real personalities.
- Talk to yourself, not as you are today, but as you were seventeen years ago.
- Talk to a future you.
- Remove yourself entirely from the conversation, and encourage a discussion between others (Lao Tzu and a dope; your accountant and Oprah; Bill Gates and a talking dog).

Although holding these imaginary dialogues can be a profitable exercise, it's not easy. For years, I read self-help books whose authors implored me to set up my own spiritual board of directors and staff it with candidates of superhuman integrity and wisdom. The idea was that I could discuss things with the people I most admired, albeit in a fabricated form.

Usually, however, after seating an imaginary Abraham Lincoln, I drew a blank on who else to draft, so all my other boardroom chairs went empty.

There I'd sit, face-to-face with the former president, rarely having the nerve to ask him my petty, simple-minded questions about career and life. At those times when I did muster the courage to speak, Lincoln's replies sounded suspiciously like the replies I'd make, spoken in my own voice.

In fact, anytime I saw a book that asked me to speak with my own fantasy advisors or, worse yet, walked me through a guided visualization during which a person, animal, or vapor would deliver profound answers to my questions, I tossed the time-wasting volume to my dogs, who gratefully pulled it apart. What, then, caused me to change my mind about the wisdom to be garnered from imaginary conversations? My forays into freewriting.

In my writing, I realized that these well-meaning authors who preached speaking to fantasized prophets perhaps had the right idea but missed the reality boat in several important ways:

- They asked me to think about my questions without asking me to write about them. My mind, therefore, wafted about and never returned with anything usable.

- They asked me to speak with someone demonstrably wiser than I am, thus scaring me into an uncreative silence. In fact, I felt guilty and disappointed because I wasn't creating anything brilliant enough for my brilliant guides to say.

- They asked me to speak to my guide in an abstract sort of way, without first fleshing out my guide as a person. I'd be addressing an abstraction instead of a vivid image, and abstractions give lousy answers.

- They didn't want me to have a conversation with my imaginary advisor as much as they wanted me to listen to the insights he delivered. This stance gave me a passive attitude to the exercise.

Through my writing, I discovered ways to make the troublesome exercise actually sing. In particular, I came up with two rules to govern my attempts at speaking with imaginary, paper counselors:

Rule #1: Put meat on the characters before making them speak.

Rule #2: Get the characters to make you speak.

Let's examine these rules, one at a time:

Put meat on the characters before making them speak.

As I alluded to previously, I have an almost obstinate inability to get my mind around an abstract concept. In school, a subject like advanced mathematics dizzied me, because I couldn't hold its ideas in my hands. ("Show me a 'function,' teacher. Where is it in our classroom?") The same thing happens with conjuring up people. To converse with a person—even one I'm partially inventing—I need to see her and understand what she's done.

If I asked you to hold an imaginary conversation with Abraham Lincoln, you'd probably hem and haw and mumble a few things about liberty. If I asked you to do two minutes of freewriting about him first, you'd probably have a slightly more fleshed-out portrait of the man, perhaps invoking the Civil War or the Gettysburg Address. If I gave you fifteen minutes, however, and asked you to write more deeply about the man, concretely picture the way he looked, and ponder the situations he worked within, you'd have quite a different conversation.

Suddenly, you might picture the weave of his long black coat, the pitch of his brow, his gnarled beard. You might hear his high, squeaky voice and smell the musky odor of the horse he'd been riding. You'd question him about the war and why Americans shot Americans.

If your mind digressed and you followed the digression, perhaps you'd remember your childhood trip to Washington,

D.C., where you saw the Lincoln Memorial. You'd tell Lincoln about the trip and ask him how he felt about his memorial and about the current state of his causes. However the conversation progressed, I'm sure you'd feel you understood Lincoln a lot better than when your thoughts of him stopped at the five-dollar bill.

At that point, too, you'd be better able to introduce your modern-day problems to him (or your fleshed-out conception of him) and hope for an interesting, perspective-changing dialogue.

What you should do, then, is engage in some method acting as you hold a conversation during your freewriting, that is, experience being in the presence of the person you're speaking to, and experience yourself as that person. Remind yourself, through your writing, to know what they might know and act as they might act.

This character-inhabiting exercise isn't as unusual as it sounds. Many novelists create dossiers about their characters, full of information that doesn't even make it into their novels. These writers, though, don't consider their attention to detail as a waste of time because they figure the more they know their characters, the more interestingly those characters will act.

How far should you go with this? It's all fantasy, so go as far as you'd like. If you know of any vocal or bodily mannerisms your character possesses, use them. If they "Ummm" a lot, make them "Ummm" on the page. If they clap their hands when they're excited, listen for sound.

Where, too, is your conversation taking place? On the phone? In person? Is Lincoln joining you for dinner? Fine, what is he having? ("Would you like a Perrier, Mr. President?") Are you taking a walk with him? Good, what's the scenery like? ("That's an airport, Mr. President.") Try talking to your character in his normal locale (Lincoln in the White House) and then in a spot you'd never associate him with

(Lincoln on a roller coaster). Perhaps meet the person over the course of a few freewriting sessions, and note where he offers you his best advice.

Get the characters to make you speak.

If you're growing uneasy about the degree of fantasy I'm asking you to entertain, this rule should calm you. It also asks you to imagine a conversation with an imaginary friend, but it more clearly recognizes the make-believe component of the exercise. Holding a paper conversation is, after all, a sham. It's a way of getting you to examine your situation through "the mind" of a consultant, astronaut, or dancer. Whatever advice you get during the exercise was actually generated by you, no matter how surprising that is. The fantasy element is effective inasmuch as it helps you get to the best parts of your mind. This "Get the characters to make you speak" rule acknowledges this, admits your mental strength, and asks your imaginary companion to act merely as a sounding board for you.

Here's another way of saying what I just said: Do the preliminary character-building writing I suggested in rule #1, but after you've clearly seen your companion, let yourself do the majority of the talking during your chat. Your companion acts as a kind of paper Socrates to your knowing-student mind, drawing fresh observations from your own lips.

→ Points to Remember

- When you hold a paper conversation, you engage in a make-believe discussion with someone and get their viewpoint on your situation.
- To hold a powerful paper discussion, you need to do two things: (1) Put meat on the character (vividly experience them in front of you), and (2) get the character to make you speak (respond to the character's brief answers and open-ended questions).

95

Try This: Think of an opportunity you'd like to investigate (changing departments, creating a new product, writing a book in your chosen field), and hold a ten-minute freewriting conversation with a paper advisor.

Now, pick out some interesting point from that conversation, and use it as a starting point for ten more minutes of writing with a different advisor.

Continue this cycle of finding a key point, conjuring up a new advisor, and doing ten more minutes of writing at least twice more.

Chapter 16

Drop Your Mind on Paper

Think of freewriting as a system of components.

Today you'll take thirty minutes to dump all the information you have about a subject onto the paper, and you'll leave it at that.

Tomorrow, you'll review your information dump and take ten minutes to write out some best-case, worst-case scenarios that stem from your previous day's efforts.

The next day, take your accumulated thoughts and free-associate for fifteen minutes, allowing the material itself to suggest new avenues to walk.

You're not pleased with your effort, so you try something else, perhaps a session in which you "open up words" and "hold a paper conversation" for twenty minutes each.

Ah, that's better. Here, among the detritus you've scattered onto the paper, are a couple of fair ideas worthy of further exploration. For some reason, though, you don't do any writing for the next three days.

Then it happens. While you're in the office listening to an on-hold version of "Eleanor Rigby," a lightbulb goes on over your head. You grab a pencil stub and a crumpled envelope and in forty seconds write a usable solution—a solution that, by the way, is a total rejection of all the ideas you had previously but needed the fertilizer of those rejected ideas to flower. In practice, that's the way freewriting works: dirty and effective. But some people thrive with a more structured approach to freewriting. They sit down regularly to write and channel their genius through a codified series of steps.

If that approach appeals to you, get your timer and your writing instruments, because we're about to deconstruct one of your problems with rigorous, scientific efficiency.

Okay, set your kitchen timer for, say, twenty minutes, and start it. In effect, you're going to take your mind and drop it onto the page in front of you. Begin to talk to yourself on the paper (or computer), starting from "try easy" and continuing to the point in your situation that has the greatest energy for you or where you feel most bugged.

Forget about making your sentences interesting. Your ideas needn't flow sequentially. Don't bother with correct grammar. And if you spell poorly, that's perfectly okay.

Start explaining to yourself why you're writing about your particular situation, and do it with the same language you'd use to speak to a smart, concerned friend who really wants to hear what you have to say.

Perhaps you might say something like:

> I'm sitting here, stupidly pounding these keys, because I've run out of good ideas on how to get more business out of the Amalgamated Pulley Corporation. They used to be my best account, but since they put in Amy as head of purchasing, I can't even get my calls returned.

Or maybe you might begin:

I said I'd do Mark a favor by trying this writing approach out, but this seems a bit nutty. Oh, well, since I told him I'd do it, let me tell myself about that portfolio situation which has me a bit confused. It seems...

If you feel resistance to addressing the situation or to this approach, write about the resistance you feel. Perhaps you want to curse. Perhaps you want to speak with yourself logically. Approach the situation from whatever perspective you choose. Do this for five minutes, or longer if necessary, putting down the facts and your reactions as fast as you can write. If you suddenly find yourself dry of words, talk to yourself on the paper about your lack of words. ("Hmm, what else can I say? Have I said it all? That's not possible. This problem's been bugging me so badly that I must think other things about it that I'm not telling. What are they? Oh, yes...") Eventually bring your mind back to your troublesome situation, even if you have to mutter to yourself about information you already put down on the page.

Now, without more than a brief glance back, write about the part of your situation that works. What's happening within it that you like? Are there people within the situation who are doing a good job of backing you up with supporting work? Have you made a number of sound decisions that have only temporarily led you to this bottleneck? Have you strengthened a skill while involved in this troublesome situation? Just where, precisely, are your thinking, behaviors, and associations working for you?

Continue your nonstriving, non-stop writing about these factors for the next few minutes. You're answering these questions, by the way, so you can examine the situation from a different perspective, not for positive thinking purposes.

Okay, you've put your situation down on paper and have briefly examined the parts that are working. Your next round of writing centers on the area where your thoughts and actions may be hurting you. If you need to scan your previous writing for a minute or so, go ahead, but don't get caught in daydreaming or rewriting. Start, instead, to talk with yourself about the areas where you've contributed to this troublesome situation.

Perhaps your actions are based on assumptions that just aren't true. Maybe you've failed to carry through on a promise you made to yourself or to others. You've probably covered some of this material during the initial step of this exercise. If so, that's fine. Just quickly note it again and continue to comb through the situation for four or five minutes for other areas where you may have dropped the ball.

At this point, your pages look like a fillet, blackened with both the logical and emotional factors that make up the situation. While writing out your thoughts, you may have even started to steer yourself toward some potential solutions. Sometimes getting all these notions and facts out of your head and down on paper is enough to trigger new, constructive associations that may have been blurred while they remained in your head.

If that's not the case, continue and ask yourself one more question: "What other situations have I seen that remind me of this one?" In reminding yourself on the page, think about similarities from situations in your own past and in others' past, as well as similarities from fictional stories you've encountered. ("My situation reminds me of that scene from *Die Hard* where Bruce Willis drops the computer down the elevator shaft.")

Such wide-ranging remembering may seem bizarre, but many top cognitive scientists, like the brilliant Roger Schank, believe it is the key to creative thought. You might also think about metaphorical images from nature, science, or art, if that'll help. ("I continually take the same course of action, kind of like birds returning to their nesting area over and over. Why do they do that, and what can I learn from them that I can use?")

Keep in mind that you're not looking for the perfect answer here. Instead, you're continuing to spray the page with possible ideas. If your situation triggers five different memories, jot them all down, even if they contradict each other. For instance, suppose you're a new consultant looking for work. Naturally, you have little (or no) consulting experience to draw on, but you've gotten jobs in other ways. Write quickly about those ways that seem most like your present situation.

If your best recollections come from nonwork situations ("This reminds me of the time I put together the yearbook in high school"), by all means scribble those situations onto the page. Don't be afraid of following the goofy, tangential stuff; it may lead somewhere important.

For the rest of the time remaining, come to some kind of conclusion, even if you must force it. Based on all the writing and thinking you've done in the past twenty minutes, what needs to be done next?

Perhaps you see a problem blockage more clearly now, and you see you don't have the technical skills to unclog it. You do, however, know a coworker with the skills to handle it. What's the best way to approach this person? When will you ask her? How will you know when the job's done effectively? If things don't go as planned, what can you do next?

Remember, you're looking for a next step, a possible solution, something to try. Of course, a few more nights of writing, done for yourself alone, may generate the kind of fresh perspectives you'll need to come up with a good solution. Usually, though, it's best to take some kind of real-world action, no matter how slight, and weave the results into the next night's writing.

This kind of writing is like the scientific method. You:

1. observe
2. hypothesize
3. experiment
4. note the results
5. ask, "What's next?"

Work until your alarm rings. (Short of a medical emergency, never quit your freewriting early!)

→ Points to Remember

- Vary the session lengths and specific techniques you use during your bouts of freewriting.
- Talk to yourself, on paper, about any resistance you're feeling about your problem or about the freewriting method itself. ("I don't feel like doing this.")
- Dumping a lot of details and information on the page often in and of itself suggests a solution.
- Let one period's writing suggest how to begin the next period's writing.
- End your writing session by telling yourself about the next real-world action you're going to take, based on your writing, even if that action is "do more writing on the subject tomorrow."

Try This: Write for twenty minutes about (1) how you're helping yourself at your job and (2) how you're hurting yourself at your job. During the writing, remind yourself of ideas and situations that seem analogous to your present situation.

Chapter 17

The Writing Marathon

A ten-minute burst of freewriting may be just what you need to solve a problem. Many times, though, you'll need longer. Instead of ten minutes, you may need six or seven hours.

Yep, I'm not kidding. Hours.

The bad part of writing nearly continuously for hours: By the end, you find yourself achy and bleary-eyed. The good part: You may have written yourself into answers that had eluded you for a lifetime.

Because this technique takes a toll on both body and mind, I use it when the stakes are high. Maybe I have to generate material for a book, competitive advantages for a client's business, or illusions for a show. A deadline invariably looms.

Here's how the writing marathon works: Fix your subject in your mind, open a blank document, set your timer for twenty minutes, and start typing.

PART TWO: POWERFUL REFINEMENTS

You're going to be writing throughout the next few hours, but that's no reason to start slow. Slow writing, in fact, is counterproductive. Keep up the pace, so your internal editor loses its grip. Ray Bradbury says, "In quickness there is truth."

When twenty minutes is up and your timer rings, stop. Now's not a time to rest. Instead, read through your twenty minutes of writing and note language and concepts that catch your attention.

If a line interests you—if it's well said or contains an idea you might want to develop—underline it. If a line strikes you as a considerable insight, bold it.

A caution: Don't overdo the underlining and bolding. If you do, nothing on the page will stand out. Note the language and thoughts you may want to revisit. Nothing more.

When you finish making annotations, look the page over once more. The reason? You want find out what to explore next.

- Do you see a thought you'd like to pursue further?
- Is there an underdeveloped idea that needs elaboration?
- Do you notice a relationship between ideas that you need to write about?
- Are you struck by a thinking error that's apparent only now that you've written it out?
- Has a question occurred to you that bears investigation?

You're searching for a starting thought, what Peter Elbow called "a center of gravity." It needn't be profound. You just want to begin writing from a spot that has energy for you—a spot that intrigues, delights, or annoys you.

Let's look at some examples of starter thoughts.

Suppose you're trying to differentiate your management consultant business. In your first twenty minutes of writing, you wrote about your services and the organizations that hire you.

As you look over the writing, you notice that although you've been hired over the years to perform a variety of services, your four favorite clients have asked you to perform the same service: large-group facilitation. That's interesting. You hadn't realized that before.

For your next twenty-minute session, then, a starter thought might be:

"What is it about large-group work that helps me attract my favorite clients?"

"How might I differentiate my business around large-group work?"

"Besides wanting large-group work, what are the similarities among my four favorite clients, and how can I use that knowledge to attract more people like them?"

"What would I be giving up if I made large-group work the focus of my business?"

These possibilities, of course, are all phrased as questions. But a starter thought can be a simple declarative statement: "I want to explore all the ways I can make large-group work the focus of my business."

Once you've come up with a starting thought, fix it in your mind, set your timer for twenty minutes, and begin writing about your starter thought.

As always, follow the dictates of your mind. If you want to stay on topic, fine. If you feel like going off topic, do it. Have fun. Be irreverent, provocative, even scandalous. Just get back to the problem you're trying to solve eventually.

When twenty minutes is up and your timer rings, stop. Again, read through your twenty minutes of writing, and underline or bold the notions that grab you. Find a new starter thought. Repeat.

That's the marathon. You do twenty-minute sessions, punctuated by the search for starter thoughts, over and over for as long as you can take it. Two hours is good. Six to seven hours is preferable. Why?

You want to clear your brain. You want it to dig deep for facts, opinions, people, stories, scenes, details, and ideas. By doing so, you'll burn off the obligatory surface thinking that can't be avoided, the party-line stuff. Your mind will have to start reaching. That's what you want.

One of the keys to making the marathon work is Ezra Pound's rallying cry, "Make it new." Each time you formulate a starter thought, demand that it sends you in a new direction. I can't stress this point enough. You don't want to merely parrot what you've already written because, if you hit "Save," you have that writing forever. Why duplicate it?

You want new. Force yourself into uncharted waters, even if doing so seems artificial or uncomfortable. Pursue novelty and uncertainty; head toward anxiety. Make yourself write and think about ideas that aren't traditionally "you." Get beyond the point where you write about what you know. As Ron Carlson wrote, "If you get what you expect, it isn't good enough."

By the end of the writing marathon, you're likely to have several solutions to try, as well as pages and pages of language and strategies you can use to help you think through other situations.

If you're interested in learning more writing marathon-like ideas, see "The Loop Writing Process" in Peter Elbow's "Writing With Power." He has wonderful thoughts on how to further disorient one's thinking so that it turns productive.

→ Points to Remember

- A brief freewriting session can help you come up with answers. To get truly fresh thoughts, however, consider conducting mini-sessions that add up to hours.
- Make sure each session begins in a new direction—even if that direction is artificial and heavy-handed.

Try This: Set aside part of a morning, and do two to three hours on an idea you'd really like to explore. During your sessions, take no phone calls and answer no e-mail.

Chapter 18

Doubt Yourself

I suffer from what a consultant friend calls "ideaphoria." That is, interesting ideas intoxicate me. In fact, I get so worked up over a good idea that my body often betrays my mind's hidden excitement; were you to peek into my study, it wouldn't be odd for you to find me rocking in my chair, slapping my leg, and mumbling feverishly to myself—all while I was guzzling a particularly heady thought.

Until now, I've allowed my public ideaphoria to gallop relatively unbridled through these pages, as I've described for you the wonders of freewriting. I've told you, yes indeed, if you regularly engage in this practice, great things may happen for you in terms of job mastery and personal satisfaction. But in my honest rush to convince you of freewriting's benefits, I may have given you the notion that such writing is one long, exhilarating slam dance of radiant ideas. If I've given you that impression, I apologize.

PART TWO: POWERFUL REFINEMENTS

Here, then, is the truth of the matter: Your freewriting may contain your thinking at its best, but it will also contain your thinking at its worst. And not only is your bad thinking on display in these writings, but your ineffectual behavior will also make many treacherous appearances, causing you to sink your head in your trembling hands.

Your freewriting, in short, will remind you time and again that you're not always as smart and productive as you believe yourself to be. (Aren't you glad you bought this book?) You'll actually find yourself growing physically and mentally tired of your own thoughts and actions.

But wait: I have life-affirming news for you! These same writings that you thought would be your ruin paradoxically hold within them your salvation. By studying those written points where your thoughts grew dry and your writing wilted, you may hit on important indicators of what and how you need to change.

This curious phenomenon of change through disgust and monotony was first put into words for me during an interview I conducted with British poet and corporate speaker David Whyte.

I know David Whyte is a poet because he can make you reevaluate your entire life while he recites a single stanza. That quality, good as it is, wouldn't put most poets in demand on the corporate speaking circuit, but Whyte is different. His telephone rings all year long with offers from multinationals who hire him to use poetry to effect change in their employees and their markets.

When Whyte takes the podium at these corporate sessions, he tries to accomplish two things: (1) get people interested in poetry and (2) get them to use poems as a way to engage in meaningful, business-centric conversation.

Let's say Whyte is called into Corporation X. He and X's managers come together and discuss a vital problem, including why the current back-and-forth isn't helping to solve things.

Based on what he hears, Whyte recites lines of poetry—from the works of Dante, Coleridge, William Carlos Williams, or any one of the hundreds of other poets whose work he's committed to memory—and leads a spirited discussion about the stalled problem, as seen through the metaphorical language of the poem. So an employee discipline problem gets run through the bracing imagery of, say, "Beowulf," and an untapped marketing opportunity gets dunked into the briny symbolism of "The Rime of the Ancient Mariner."

Suddenly, the people at Corporation X are discussing the problem in a way they never thought possible, and coming, hopefully, to an understanding that will translate itself into a workable business practice. Of the reactions his intervention gets, Whyte says, "People get excited when they have language for qualities and phenomena they didn't previously have. These people now have language for going into difficult places."

Whyte, in a sense, channels the wisdom of dead poets as a way to create an atmosphere of possibility in the bottom-line world of the twenty-first-century corporate worker. He understands that even complex global problems can be solved when people start speaking in ways just slightly differently than they're used to speaking.

So why am I telling you this?

Just as Whyte has firsthand experience that novel language and images force workers into fresh perspectives, he's also seen that stereotyped change motivations aren't always the most effective ways to generate change. He revealed this to me, in an aside, while I was interviewing him about writing poetry:

Me: You have a love of many poets, of people like Coleridge, yet you want to write like yourself. How do you stop all these loves from interfering with your unique writing voice?

Whyte: You start with imitation because you don't know how to do this [produce a poem]. These poets are doing astonishing things. So you find the ones you love—there's absolutely nothing wrong with writing pieces that are pure Ted Hughes or Seamus Heaney or Rilke—and you just keep writing your way into your own voice. Eventually, you realize that you're not writing Rilke or Heaney anymore, that there's another voice there which you, in Mary Oliver's words, "slowly recognize as your own."

That's actually a well recognized way of discovering your own voice—of imitating others until you get tired of imitating others.

A lot of the poetic discipline boils down to getting tired of yourself, and I really believe that. When you get tired of yourself, then you change. See, even if you're stuck in life, if you can describe just exactly the way you're stuck, then you will immediately recognize that you can't go on that way anymore. So, just saying precisely, writing precisely how you're stuck, or how you're alienated, opens up a door of freedom for you.

Whyte's language choices sent gonglike reverberations through my head. "Tired," "stuck," and "alienated" are not the usual motivational words businesspeople use when doping out their slick methodologies for change, but Whyte used them. These words seemed so unheroic, so petty, so selfish, but so true! So the question becomes, How can we identify—and deal with productively—those tired elements in our own work lives?

Based on my own freewriting, and on that of students who have shared their work with me, here are a few hiding places for tiredness that you might like to investigate in your own jotting:

- You keep harking back to the same thoughts ("I really should finish X").
- ...the same people ("Janet is the key to finding a way out of this").
- ...the same images or metaphors ("The market is like a deodorant stick").
- ...the same language (you riddle a page with the phrase "buckle down" forty-two times).

- You race past ordinary yet distasteful scenes as quickly as you can ("I completed all my rancid paperwork today").
- You're continually self-critical ("I obviously stink").
- You're continually other-critical ("Barney obviously stinks").
- You believe you've tried out all possible solutions, and they've all left you wanting ("That's the tenth and final way that I know won't work").
- You assume that nothing can be done about a specific situation ("It's hopeless").
- While reading your work aloud (to yourself), your voice inexplicably hesitates or wavers at passage X.

Now, please don't eyeball a page or two of your freewriting, notice one of these symptoms, and exclaim, "Zounds! I knew it! I am tired!" Or worse yet, start a fresh page of writing in which you "unintentionally" shoehorn in one or more of these symptoms and stun yourself with revelation.

Growing tired of yourself isn't a technique to practice, like calling a new prospect by his first name throughout the sales call. Instead, its value is in knowing that it exists—and it may be hiding out in the open, because you've been ignoring its song.

If you find tiredness's droppings, note how they've been deposited into your life. If those droppings don't make themselves plain on the page, don't crawl on your hands and knees trying to sniff them out.

So what is to be done if you find one of these symptoms or, perhaps, one I've neglected to mention? At first, nothing. Becoming tired, bored, and disgusted with your situation is part of your nature, hardwired into you by divinity, evolution, or both. At times, the best way to deal with being tired is to let yourself be tired.

How, though, do you tell if your writing reveals points of destructive tiredness or constructive plateauing? Back to David Whyte for the answer.

If you recall, he said:

See, even if you're stuck in life, if you can describe just exactly the way you're stuck, then you will immediately recognize that you can't go on that way anymore. So, just saying precisely, writing precisely how you're stuck, or how you're alienated, opens up a door of freedom for you.

Tattoo that word "exactly" into your mind. It's the freewriter's best friend. If you put into words exactly how the project failed, exactly how the negotiations faltered, exactly how your career stumbled, magic happens. A lucidity creeps into your thinking; this lucidity may come only with several trips to the well of exact writing, but it clears your head like a window thrown open.

Your head-clearing lucidity may point you in a number of directions. Maybe it will tell you, yes, you're tired of situation X, things need to change, and here's a protoplan. Or based on what's come before, it may tell you that you're stepping across a mucky plateau, and the only thing that's needed is to push gamely ahead. How, though, do you cast this spell known as "exact writing"?

→ Points to Remember

- If you put honest thinking into your written words, you spot situations that yawn to be changed.

Try This: Write for ten minutes about a situation that physically and mentally exhausts you. Don't try to solve anything in this bout of writing; just get the details down.

Chapter 19

The Magic of Exact Writing

I could ask you right now to put into words exactly how you're tired or precisely how you're stuck. And if I asked you to do that, do you know what you'd put on the page? Fairy tales.

To ask you to talk about your situation—with exacting, surgical precision—is just about as impossible as drawing a foot-wide circle on the ground and asking a skydiver to hit it.

First, you can never know your own motivations for certain, much less know the motivations of others.

Second, growing tired happens over time; to ask you to make a summarizing statement about a fairly long-standing, meandering problem would be ludicrous.

Third, to ask you to boil down your situation would rob you of the very way out of it: churning it over in your mind, from different angles, so that myriad previously unseen perspectives suddenly lie exposed to the light.

The way, then, to write "exactly" about being tired isn't

the impossible work of parsing your thoughts into one cutting laser beam of accuracy. Instead, it's about dumping eighteen pounds of words onto paper and making sure you're living those words as you write them.

Here's the same answer, rendered clearer through anecdote: Back in the mid-1960s, before even a sentence from *The Right Stuff* or *Bonfire of the Vanities* ever flashed inside his mind, Tom Wolfe was struggling for a way to approach a particularly unconventional magazine article he longed to write.

Wolfe wanted to profile a hot rod and custom car designer who soberly, and artistically, approached his freak show craft. Wolfe knew this was an important human interest story and societal critique, but he didn't know how to coax it into words.

With the magazine's deadline about to steamroll him, Wolfe called his editor and came clean about his tired, hopeless state. About that conversation, Wolfe writes:

> O.K., he [the magazine's editor] tells me, just type out my notes and send them over and he will get somebody else to write it. So about 8 o'clock that night I started typing the notes out in the form of a memorandum that began, "Dear Byron" [his editor's name]. I started typing away, starting right with the first time I saw any custom cars in California. I just started recording it all, and inside of a couple of hours, typing like a madman, I could tell something was happening.... The details themselves, when I wrote them down, suddenly made me see what was happening.

After a marathon eight-and-a-half-hour, uncensored writing session, a sleepless Wolfe took his "notes" over to the magazine, where they promptly scratched the "Dear Byron" salutation and published the entire forty-nine pages (rather than the two-page article it was supposed to be). Thus began the distinctive style of one of the world's finest writers.

To us, of course, the publishing success part of the story is unimportant. What we do need to pay attention to is Wolfe's manic, non-stop writing style and the principles he used to make that style fly. Of particular note, let's examine Wolfe's audience for the memorandum, his use of the phrase "recording it all," and his attention to detail.

The Audience

By "audience," I mean the person to whom Wolfe addressed the memorandum, Byron Dobell, the managing editor at *Esquire* magazine. Now, should you address your own writings to Mr. Dobell, or to other prominent editors, in the hope that your style will set a brushfire through the literary world and burn all the way up the best-seller lists? (It's okay if you answered yes, although for the sake of the lesson, let's assume you answered no.) For the most part, other than yourself, you'll have no audience for your writing—and that's the way it should be. Your freewriting is confidential, for your eyes only, and you should strike out with fists and feet at anyone who feels the need to sneak a peek at your thoughts. (If you want to make part of it public, that's something to decide later.)

But what if you tried directing your thoughts toward someone else, even if this "someone else" never saw your writing? Do you think such a mind game would affect the direction of your ideas? You'd better believe it would!

Try this: Fix a subject in your mind, a subject about which you consider yourself an expert. Now, if I asked you to give a 250-second speech about it to a roomful of surgeons, how might you tailor the information to make it interesting to them? Even if the material doesn't lend itself to overt customization—how would I apply my origami expertise to cardiologists?—the fact that you'll be speaking to a highly educated group certainly alters the way you'd talk. (I can use words like "laity" and "recalcitrant.")

Now give your speech to a roomful of high school students. Certainly, high school students can be as smart as the proverbial whip, but you couldn't possibly deliver your surgeon-specific speech to a roomful of youngsters, could you? You'd have to recast what you say. And by altering what you do and say, you'd be thinking about your material in a different way, based on the characteristics of the audience.

Consider, then, this idea of varying audience in your own writing, particularly as you try to write precisely about a tired situation (almost like holding a paper conversation, except your audience remains silent but attentive). Wolfe certainly saw his material through new eyes, as the magnetic force of "Dear Byron" exerted its steady pull on his thought selection. The act of freewriting may start crunching some fresh creases into your brain if that writing is directed in a never-to-be-sent letter to your boss, spouse, friend, enemy, controller, salesperson, marketer, warehouse employee, janitor, favorite actor, hated actor, or a figure in history. If you make an honest effort to alter your audience as an experiment, you can't help writing yourself into some unexplored perspectives.

Recording It All

Because Wolfe was uncertain about how to shape his material, and because he didn't know what was critical and what was marginal, he spewed everything he could recall about the story down on paper (forty-nine sheets' worth, remember?). To use his own words, he "recorded it all." Now what did Wolfe mean by invoking the word "recorded"? When I think of that word, I get a picture of an accountant dutifully entering a number in a large, brown leather ledger, with no judgments or pondering, just hand movement. And that's exactly what I think Wolfe did and what I'd like you to do. While you're examining your tired situation, "record," or put on the page, everything that pops into your mind, whether it

116

seems germane to the problem or not. If you want to judge what you're recording, by all means do it, but do it without crossing out what you've written, criticizing yourself without questioning why you deserve that criticism, or stopping to phrase your thoughts more appropriately.

Think of "recording it all" as a heuristic that encourages you to articulate the unarticulated. In the same way that it's not up to the accountant to alter the number she's entering because she doesn't approve of that number, it's also not up to you to alter your thoughts as they appear. Disapprove of them, if you like, in the next sentence from your pen, but don't banish them to the vapors of the unsaid.

Details

So far I've told you that, according to David Whyte, describing "exactly" a situation that's mentally exhausted you will help you change the situation, either through your attention to its workings, by your acceptance of its existence, or via the overt change strategies you create to break it up. I've also told you, by examining Tom Wolfe's approach to a similar problem, that the way to write "precisely" about your situation is not through careful, edited language, but by choosing fresh audiences to help draw fresh perspectives from you and by recording all thoughts as they burst into your consciousness. Now I'll explain that the most telling thing you'll find in the Wolfe excerpt is the sentence "The details themselves, when I wrote them down, suddenly made me see what was happening."

Details get a bad rap. When we say, "Attend to the details," it's said almost as a rebuke, as a caution to keep our minds on our work and not foul things up as we've done in the past. But looking at things closely reveals a paradoxical simplicity and complexity that makes almost anything fascinating, if not beautiful.

PART TWO: POWERFUL REFINEMENTS

That last statement, abstract enough to float off the page like a lost balloon, needs to be brought back to earth. Let me make that point this way: Say you serve as a marketer for a publisher, and one of your jobs is to e-mail your accounts about upcoming media appearances for your company's books. That sounds important, but most of the information you normally send is bland stuff, a brief title mention in a regional newspaper or an author's late-night radio appearance. Consequently, you drag your Internet-driven heels and turn to other projects rather than attend to the detail it takes to put together a credible e-mail. Your inaction eventually breeds more inaction, until you find yourself incapable of clicking your mouse.

During a spirited session of freewriting, you address this tired issue, calling it "a barbell that cuts into my shoulders, and weighs me down all the day long." As a kind of experiment, you decide that since your company's books aren't getting more interesting and your authors aren't becoming more newsworthy, you'll research ways to spice up your e-mails and create some kind of value for you and your customers.

You hit the bookstore, the library, and the Web, scoring a handful of texts on how to add zing to your electronic communiqués. Pen at the ready, you underline information on how to grab reader interest and sustain it throughout the letter. After blowing through a stack of scrap paper, you put together a letter that's better than your standard attempts. You send it and do some follow-up. Not everyone has read your letter, but some people have. You talk to these people and find out about the kinds of information they need to make a success of your company's books.

One of the store owners clues you in to several chat rooms centered around the subjects your company's books are noted for: Perhaps you could investigate some direct marketing to these groups. You're off to buy new books, make calls, and perform experiments.

Through your freewriting and your real-life experience, you're discovering that you'd stopped paying attention to your tired situation in any meaningful way; you had, in your mind, filed it under "bore," and there it stayed. By getting into the details of what bored you and how you might possibly use that boredom as a starting point for a new direction, you've made that situation come alive again, only this time you're making it work for you.

Have I made it clear, then, that writing in detail about anything elevates the subject out of the abstract class (such as automobile) and into a hard nuts-and-bolts reality where our minds can rap their mental knuckles against it (a red Firebird, with black leather seats, and a small American flag on the antenna snapping in the wind)?

Before you turn on your laptop and do freewriting about this chapter, here's a brief checklist of suggestions that you may want to play around with in "exact" writing:

- Start your writing at the spot in the problem that most befuddles you. Ask yourself, why is there blockage here?

- Record your current thoughts about the situation, as well as your thoughts when the situation first arose. How do they differ and why?

- Mentally peruse the situation and see if you've included everyone who belongs in it.

- When you're trying to analyze the behavior of others, stick to writing about their observable behavior; although we often believe we know what others are thinking, we don't.

- If you're having trouble reliving the situation on paper, follow the wise advice of Peter Elbow, who tells his students: "To hell with words, see something." What Elbow means is to put yourself into the experience as vividly as you can. What counts is that you see, hear, touch, smell, and taste the situations you're visiting and that you render those strong experiences in the most vivid, concrete language you have. Perhaps now, given your freewriting-induced perspectives on things, you'll find a possible answer that eluded you initially.

- Don't assume your tired situation is something to be "solved." It may be necessary to play it out as it stands. Or it may fix itself.
- Question whether you've really tried a certain solution or whether you just think you know how it would turn out. We often think we've tried things that our minds have prematurely discounted.

→ Points to Remember

- Exact writing—that is, getting to the very heart of an important matter—requires you to flood the paper with words that honestly and graphically depict what you're thinking, seeing, and feeling about the matter. Exhaust yourself during the writing, in the hope that a few of your words ring true and suggest a solution.
- Use a variety of people as a focusing force in your writing.
- The most reliable way to be honest in your writing is to use lots of physical detail and kitcheny descriptions of what you're thinking. If your mind tells you to write X, write X, even if writing Y would have made more logical sense.

Try This: Write for ten minutes about a crappy situation, but before you begin, address the page to someone involved in the difficulty (such as "Dear Sharon"). Write to the person in exacting detail, dumping as much information on the page as you can. When the timer rings, do another ten minutes of writing about the crappy situation, only this time address your remarks to someone who's involved in one of your cool situations. See if focusing on this person gives you a different view of the tough situation.

Chapter 20

Extract Gold from a Business Book

In this chapter, you'll be learning how to study a business book and make its potentially valuable concepts your own by agreeing and arguing with them on your freewriting paper. If the book's ideas are strong, you'll have a greater sense of ownership of them, even knowing how to test them out in your own life. If the book's ideas stink, then you'll gain by refuting those ideas. You must actively engage with the material and make it move. That's a key to this chapter, this book, and this approach.

Okay, you need a business book with a premise that intrigues you, one you'll want to give a close reading. There's no sense in torturing yourself with a work repellent to you. As you work your way through the book, doctor its innards with your underlining and private notations. Don't respect the book as a physical object. Customize it. When you come to a sentence that stops you, a paragraph that makes you think, or a fact that you may want to consult, highlight it in some way so you can easily put your finger on it again.

What you're doing here is corralling material that resonates to you, that sets your "spider sense" tingling. You're ticking off pieces of the book that strike you as out of the ordinary. Also, your ever-circling pen is keeping you alert and forcing you to pay attention to the author's ideas, even if the prose style may not justify it.

If, while reading, you have questions you'd like to ask the author, write them in the book's margin. The same thing goes for an insight. Don't wait to put your thought into words, assuming that it's so $E=mc^2$-brilliant that you'll retain it in your mind forever. You won't. Rather, scribble it onto the page, even if you have to obscure the original text to do so. Don't, by the way, be stingy with your underlining, because if you don't save the book's vibrant material now, it'll be dead to you once you shut the cover. I'm being realistic. There's too much to read, learn, and do in this life, and unless a volume stands out as particularly worthy, you'll probably only thumb through it again to consult your highlights. The rest of the text might as well not be there.

At some point during this customizing process, you'll have a book containing thousands of words that mean nothing to you, and a few words that warrant some follow-up cogitating. Perhaps you'll want to read through the entire book before engaging in freewriting. More than likely, though, your opinion-generating glands will start secreting as soon as you come across an interesting topic and force you to forsake the reading temporarily. By all means, give in: Strip the intriguing piece of prose from the text or encapsulate it in your own words, slap it on your computer screen, and bang out ten to twenty minutes of non-stop opinion and excitement.

Let me give you an example of what I'm talking about. I've opened my own electronic freewriting file on William J. Hudson's *Intellectual Capital*, and I'm paging through ten screens, expressing my intrigue, delight, and occasional consternation with Hudson's views. Here's one passage that spoke to me and my answer to it:

> It is a false hope that the world can be simplified into a handful of discrete propositions called trends or megatrends. The world is simply not obligated to do this. It need not kneel to human intelligence. And to believe that you can come to possess "master ideas" may blind you to what you can do, which is barely outdistance your competitors (in the nick of time).

What is Hudson saying here? I think it's this: The world is ridiculously (yet appropriately) knotted-full of processes that function in tension against each other. For us to think we can sum up such a complex system in a few words (the very basis of a megatrend) is a grand display of hubris, and must be inaccurate.

These processes don't slow down or simplify so we can study and classify them. They proceed in the way that they proceed. Some things in this life just aren't comprehensible; that doesn't mean we should give up attempts to grasp our world, or swallow back all pronouncements and grand projections; it's just that we should be aware that our pronouncements are almost certainly screening us from most of the picture.

In this Hudson excerpt, he finishes by saying "what we can do" is "barely outdistance" competitors. What he means here, if I'm reading this correctly, is that once we realize that megatrends do as much to blind us as to what's happening, we can still use the knowledge and judgment we have to get done what we need to, just before our competitors beat us to it.

Could Hudson be wrong here? It's hard for me to argue against him.

I've always felt that people who make long-term predictions were basically writing fiction in public, but doing it under the guise of telling the truth. The best way to argue against Hudson is to say this: if you declare a trend, even to yourself, and work to make it happen, it could happen—and in that way, it helps, as a generating tool. If I say that I see more people are going to the theater, and I build a theater to capitalize on this trend, and work my kishkas off getting people into that theater and make it successful, then I guess my pronouncement would be a kind of self-fulfilling prophecy. A creative delusion that works to help me. Something to strive toward.

How could I use this idea in my own life? Not every idea needs to have immediate, practical use. But if I put some effort into seeing it with pragmatic specs, then maybe I'll have an easier time remembering it when it might come in handy. My answer, then: I don't go around announcing trends, but maybe I sometimes act on the world as if certain trends, or shall I call them assumptions, are true.

I know, for instance, if a certain sales account of mine has a history of giving me a two hundred dollar order, I think of them as a two hundred dollar account, and treat them accordingly—small-time: I'm not as forthcoming with special information, I may not stay as late as I should to help them, etc. My actions, in effect, are guaranteeing the growth of this account stay stunted. If I combed my client list and noted where I'm working to keep revenues small, I could try experimenting by giving these accounts a two thousand dollar effort. I get the feeling I'm trying to turn Hudson's words into a self-help concept here, rather than using them to deal with the world at large, which is what he intended. But let me just remind myself that trend-watchers and I both think we have the world's number, we know how it'll behave, and our assumptions and projections might just be flat-out wrong.

Another example? Here, then, is my attempt to bring some personal meaning to a paragraph culled from Philip Crosby's book, *The Absolutes of Leadership:*

If quality is defined in more traditional words such as "goodness" and "delight," no one knows what it means. Quality then becomes an "I know it when I see it" kind of thing. People will argue about how good something has to be. It is much better to have people discuss requirements and deal with specifics rather than emotions.

I know there's been a lot of debate about "quality," and about the validity of that practice (Wow, I sound formal. Certain subjects draw that voice out). Malcolm Baldrige Award–winning companies have even gone out of business, only years after having proved that they were mandarins of quality control. But Crosby has a solid point in stating people should deal in "specifics rather than emotions" (emotions, though, is an unfortunate word choice here; emotions often have a lot to do with the specifics of what's recognized as quality).

As long as people stay with flabby generalities ("I like this way of doing business because it's good"), there's nothing to discuss or work with. So too, if I say something ambiguous, like "Process X should be done faster," that's only a starting point for improving Process X.

Some meaningful questions accompanying "Process X should be done faster" would be provocations like, "Faster? How much faster? What would faster look like to you? Why does it need to go faster? Would going faster be something our customers would notice? Would going faster in Process X pull resources away from another part of our business and damage us there? What if we dropped Process X altogether? Would an improvement in Process X have a beneficial carry-over effect to any of our other processes? How would we make Process X faster? What are ten different ways we could make Process X better? Which of these ten answers holds the most promise, and why? If we applied one of these answers, how would we know if it was working? How would we decide to keep this new method as a regular part of Process X? If we had to excise our 'improvement' out of Process X, would we have to explain its removal to our customers? If we did remove this 'improvement,' how would we explain our decision to others? If this improvement worked, how could we leverage it and use it in other parts of our business?"

I hear you, with eyes bulged in fear (or boredom), asking yourself, "Is Mark actually going to answer all these questions?" Of course not.

The point here is not to make unnecessary work for ourselves by manufacturing endless questions. The point is to know that all these questions can rightfully be asked, and most of them should be asked, even if they generate only a one- or two-sentence response. The rule to follow is this: During freewriting, always wrestle with a subject where it holds the most energy for you.

If, in your own writing, you formulate a question that excites you, take off after it like a dog after a rabbit. You can always look back after your sprint and fill in those yeoman parts of your quest that need filling in. That's part of the beauty of using writing to help you figure out problems: The writing doesn't withdraw after it flashes on the page. Don't make your task grim. These freewriting moments should be among the most invigorating of your day, like rubbing down your mind with a rough towel.

Back to my freewriting:

All this talk of requirements and specifics is hunky-dory, but a full-scale, consultant-driven quality intervention is not going to happen where I work. I remember years back bringing in Crosby's people for a look-see at our place, but the bosses didn't think it warranted the expense. And maybe they were right.

How, though, can I suck the marrow out of these quality bones? How can I apply the good information in this excerpt to what I do?

Well, on a sales level, I can bug my customers about what constitutes quality in their dealings with me. What specifics cause them to say, "Mark and his company are outstanding," and what specifics cause them to say, "I wish Mark and his company did this better."

Better write up a checklist of subjects to talk about with my clients, since people might forget to tell me about a specific that doesn't jump readily to mind. What would be on my checklist?

Sales: Do we speak often enough? Too often? Do I bring up the necessary books and information? What else could I be doing for them? What do other companies do for them? Are our terms good?

Shipping: Do our books get to their stores when they expect them to arrive? Is this quick enough? Are our boxes sturdy? Is the packing material doing its job? Are the invoices clear?

Marketing: Do they need materials from us? Are they aware of all the co-op policies out there, and are they taking advantage of them? Do they ever access our Web page, and does it have anything on it they can use?

Accounting: Are we helpful and easy to deal with?

Obviously, I'll need to talk with the heads of other departments before conducting my little survey. I'm sure there are important questions I should be asking, but haven't thought of (Yes, returns!). I'll also make it a point to try and get my clients to give me stories about good and bad service they've received from us. Sometimes, a vivid story reveals more than a list of properties divorced from a flesh-and-blood situation.

Notice how I took a concept, largely unusable from where I stood in my organization, and extracted as much as I could from it.

After debating with the Crosby excerpt, I had something of an understanding of what he was getting at (although Crosby himself may dispute that); more important, I had a plan of action based on the ideas I had dissected. Yes, I did go through with the plan you see written here, it did generate results, and I tracked those results on the home field of my freewriting page.

→ Points to Remember

- Customize business books as you read them: underline, dog-ear, question, argue, agree vehemently, write in the margins and on the blank end papers. You're reading the book to get workable ideas, and the best way to find the workable ideas is to be active as you read.

- Through writing, try applying the author's ideas to your own life. Even if you disagree with what the author says, that disagreement suggests that you know what should be done. Write about this knowing.

Try This: Pick the most valuable idea and the least valuable idea in this book, and write for ten minutes on each.

Chapter 21

You Are What You Focus On

This chapter might not seem to be about writing, but it is.

While still in my teens, I came across a quote that has stuck with me. The words were Emerson's, and the philosopher had written, "Make the most of yourself, for that is all there is of you."

In my gangly enthusiasm, I neatly copied those words onto an index card, carefully folded the card into quarters, and carried it as a sort of literary smelling salts, to be inhaled when I needed a rush of pragmatic bravado for those situations in which I felt overmatched.

I wish I could tell you that the quote radically altered my life, that Emerson's spirit blew hot across the centuries, filling my lungs with his transcendental fury, but it didn't. I probably tossed the index card when my wallet became too fat to sit on.

But here's how the spirit of the quote did stick and how

it helped me work gradually toward the things I find important: Emerson's words marked the first time I realized that if I was ever going to do anything that mattered with my life, I had to use whatever fixed mental and physical capacities I was born with. That is, unless I put in effort, I wasn't going to suddenly become smarter, more athletic, or a greater success at anything.

Emerson's words also signified the first time I started valuing the contents of my mind—not because my intellect was a raging force of nature that leveled anything in its path, but because, again, that's what I had been given to work with.

I realized that if I wanted to write books, I had to be the type of person who focused on book-writing types of activities (reading, grammar, journalistic techniques, etc.). If I wanted to be a salesman, I had to focus on sales-type activities (prospecting, getting favorable attention, establishing rapport, etc.). The skills I needed weren't going to drop on me while I slept, like benevolent airborne spores. I had to focus on them.

My focus, in a sense, has defined who I am. Because I've paid so much attention to the publishing field, I haven't become, for instance, a landscape architect or a baseball player. Because I enjoy using my leisure time to study magic, I spend little time studying stamp collecting or knife throwing. My particular focus has other crucial implications for my life. Not only does my attention dictate what subjects I spend my time and effort investigating, it also tells me how I should investigate them. Geoff Bellman, an astute management consultant, expressed this thought beautifully when he wrote:

> Having spent my early years in a training department, I
> was disposed to think of performance problems as training
> problems. Especially in the realm of management behavior
> or interpersonal behavior, I "knew" that if someone was not

doing something very well, it was because he or she didn't know how and merely needed training. And of course, I was a trainer, so wasn't that nice for both of us? Not surprisingly, now that I don't do much training anymore, I see it differently.

I, too, approach situations wielding my own focus-based biases. Rather than beginning with an open-minded view of a problem, I suspect that my mind starts me at a favorite, rut-worn set point and sends me searching for solutions from there.

All my talk of focus, so far, sounds overtly ominous, with its life-changing paths taken and ignored. Focus, however, decrees what I see, or don't see, even in mundane ways.

Just the other day I realized there was a Post-it note stuck to the edge of my workplace computer screen. Now, this note didn't suddenly erupt all by itself. I stuck it there myself, fourteen months earlier.

I had this note in my line of sight more than forty hours a week, week after week, and I focused on it only when I inadvertently jostled my terminal. For whatever reasons, Post-it notes don't interest me, at least not those on the rim of my computer screen.

I, in some ways, know how I operate, and I "know" that if that Post-it note had critical information on it, I would have stuck it in the center of the computer screen or on the keyboard keys. If something really needs to be done, I want it to get in my way, to hound me, to stay in the center ring of my attending mind.

This poor curling Post-it, which had seen spring turn to winter, and winter turn to summer, and its penciled message—"Get videotapes and books back from David"—was potent enough that I didn't want to forget it but mild enough that it never pushed me across the threshold of action. For approximately four hundred working days, then, my focus looked past that Post-it and told me there were more important things to attend to.

PART TWO: POWERFUL REFINEMENTS

Do these focus-related thoughts of mine get a smile of recognition from you, or are you mentally tossing them to the floor and stubbing them out with your heel? Although I've yet to let you get a word in this chapter, my focus certainly hasn't left you. If you and I were sitting together in a room right now, I would ask you to relate your stories, big and small, regarding focus. You might tell me what you do for a living, what your hobbies are, what your family life is like. We'd order pizza. You'd continue by telling me what gets you fired-up mad and switched-on happy. I'd ask what part you thought your private focus played in these matters, and whether altering your focus would alter the way you lived your life. I'd study your words, and your excitement, for proof that this concept had "taken" in your mind, that you believed it fully. Whether I sensed that you believed it or not, I'd offer up one small exercise, a kind of magic trick, to give you the experience of attention alteration while we were sitting there.

Since obviously we aren't sitting together, I can't come through on our conversation or the pizza. But what I can do is give you a visceral demonstration of focus by asking you to participate in a small trick, a magical experience.

Without looking up from this page, mentally create a list of all the red objects in the room. Please, stop and do this now.

Now look around you. How many red objects do you see? Before you started reading this page, your focus wasn't on red objects, so you didn't notice them. But when you focused on them, you picked out quite a few from your surroundings.

Let's go a step further. Suppose I tell you that I'll pay you $1,000 for a list of 100 red objects in the room. Talk about attention and focus! Chances are, given my (fictitious) challenge, you'd not only catalogue all the obvious red objects, but you'd develop a creative streak worthy of James Joyce

132

to flesh out the list: "If I unscrew my telephone receiver, I see red wires. If I jab my finger with this paper clip, I see red blood. If I break down my red bookcase into its components, I have six red shelves."

Is this a small trick or a magical experience? If you actually participated in the exercise, I'm sure you received a delightful jolt in discovering just how "evasive" objects are, even as they sit, unmoving, in your line of vision. This idea—seeing what's in front of you, be it hidden ideas or unnoticed objects—will run strongly through much of the work you'll do once you close this book. In a sense, I think you'll find that you discover what you search for, and that without your active effort in the search, an important idea or resource might as well not be there at all.

→ Points to Remember

- What we focus on, in large part, determines how we lead our lives.
- Use your freewriting to keep your focus on what you want to make of your life. (Sometimes, the things we find most crucial for a great life get buried under the rigors of daily existence.)

Try This: Set your timer for twenty minutes, and start it. Tell yourself in freewriting everything you currently think of as necessary for a superior life. Include material and non-material criteria. Make sure you take away at least one item from that list that you'll act on in the next three hours.

Part Three

Going Public

For freewriting to be effective, you must assume that, during any single session, no one but you will see what you've written. After all, it's the private element that helps you put on paper exactly what's on your mind.

That said, you can and should use ideas and prose culled from your freewriting over the course of time for public documents, like blogs and books. This section gives you some tips on how.

Chapter 22

Sharing Your Unfinished Thoughts

In 1998 or 1999, I got the idea for what became the original edition of *Accidental Genius.* To entice publishers, I had to write a book proposal. The thought of penning a proposal for a book I hadn't yet started work on intimidated me.

The proposal had to be comprehensive and persuasive. It needed to give publishers the impression that I already knew everything there was to know about the book and how it would sell.

In the proposal, I'd have to talk about the work's premise and how I'd substantiate it. I'd have to discuss how it would unfold, from first page to last. I'd have to predict which markets would buy it and why. I'd have to analyze the competitive landscape: What books out there were similar, and how would mine be different? I'd have to lay out a marketing plan that demonstrated how I'd throw my all into pushing the book. I'd have to talk about my background and why

PART THREE: GOING PUBLIC

I was the perfect person to write the book. As a capper, I'd have to include a couple of sample chapters, showing that I wasn't just mouthing off and could, indeed, deliver an engaging read.

The proposal needed to be a bulky sixty to ninety pages. Anything less, a proposal-writing book assured me, and publishers would assume my idea would work better as a magazine article. Anything more and they'd assume I was unfocused.

I didn't know where to begin, so I phoned my agent, Karl Weber. I still remember the calm that enveloped me during the call. When it began, my insides were clenched. When it was over, I couldn't wait to produce what he had asked for.

Karl said that for the moment I should forget about the proposal. Instead, I was to write him a letter. He called it a talking letter. He asked me to write down anything that came to mind about what I wanted the book to be, and how I thought I could help sell it. My letter was supposed to be nothing formal, not an act of literature, just one friend to another, talking.

Writing that letter was freedom. Much as Tom Wolfe had done when writing up his notes for Byron Dobell (Chapter 19), I typed "Dear Karl" at the top of a page, and let it pour: facts, anecdotes, ideas, and fears. The letter took me a few hours to compose. Now we had something to discuss. A starting point. Over the course of a few weeks, Karl and I turned what I had written into a proposal for a book that got bought.

There's benefit in articulating what you're thinking and feeling, even if you're not 100 percent sure what you're thinking and feeling. There's also benefit in sharing your unfinished thoughts.

Creating a document to pass around gives helpful form to your rough thinking; it gives people something tangible to react to. The feedback will be useful, and so will the energy and thought you put into creating it.

What Karl called a talking letter, I've since called by different names, including a pass-around document and a collage document. I now call it a "talking document" (a radical change, I know). A talking document is a problem-solving document. It shows where your mind is headed without fully committing to anything. You're not showing off, and you need no definite answers. The document is easy to create.

One way of doing it is as Karl advised me. Write it as a letter to a real person. Who? Someone you trust, who's on your side, cares about what you think, and wants the best for you. Try, if possible, to write to someone involved in the project you're brainstorming. That way, they'll give informed comments. But if there's no one you can write to who is part of the project, write to a trusted outsider.

Should you contact the person ahead of time and tell them about the letter you'll be sending? I do. I check to make sure they want to help, have time to read the letter, and understand what I expect, which is feedback on what they find good, bad, or interesting.

I've never had someone turn me down, but if they did, I wouldn't go ahead and write the letter to them as a kind of thought experiment. Doing that would provide me with only half the benefit. Thinking things through so another person can understand you is one beneficial half. Using those thoughts to fuel a real conversation is the other half. If the person I approached turned me down, I'd find someone else.

You can also address the letter to a group. Of course, that complicates things. You've got to know and feel safe with all the members of the group.

So a straightforward letter format is one way of creating a talking document. A second way is to construct it as a freestyle collage. Such an approach often produces a richer result. You're able to draw on some of your freewriting, and the writing of others, without having to knit it all together seamlessly. You can let the gaps in the story show.

PART THREE: GOING PUBLIC

How would you make a collage-style thinking document? Start the way you would with the letter-style method by getting in mind a person whose ethics and thinking you trust. That person can be a friend, a colleague, a client.

You'd then do a series of freewriting sessions about the situation in question. As always, you'd attack your subject from as many angles as you'd like: information dumps, fanciful digressions, bad ideas, good ideas, opening up words, paper conversations, scenes that struck you, worst-case scenarios, best-case scenarios. Wherever you want to go, use the writing to go there. Write with abandon, because no one, not even your trusted reader, will see everything you've written.

Once you've said what you have to say, strip away all the language that's dead, blue, or insane, leaving the stuff that works. Rearrange those chunks in an order that makes sense to you. Don't worry if you can't articulate why you arranged them that way. Collage is more creation by gut than creation by logic.

Now, add anything you'd like to the collage. Do extra writing and graft it onto the document. Add prose from other writers, such as reporters or bloggers (making sure, of course, to point out whose writing this is). Put in snippets of interviews you've done, strategies you've tried, hypotheses you've concocted, photos you've taken, graphs you've drawn. Anything at all that feels like it might shed light on your idea, put it in.

Read the document through. Here's where you can put in transitions. Either use words to show the progression of the material (such as "First," "Second," "Third") or use extra line breaks or rows of asterisks to show where sections begin and end. Again, don't worry if things flow or make air-tight sense.

Once you've done that, write the beginning. Address your reader, and say what you're up to. Touch on the prob-

140

lem you've been thinking about and where your thinking is headed. Tell them what you'd like from them in terms of counsel. Let them know, too, that the document they're about to read may not make perfect linear sense, but it does contain many of the ideas you've been wrestling with.

Proofread it and send it.

The person you sent it to can comment within the document or create another document in response. The two of you can also use your writing to help create short homemade video responses ("I know the brainstorm is happening in three days, but here's what I'm thinking...") or use other creative ways to get and keep the conversation going.

Would you like to see what a collage might look like? Here is a piece of one where I've disguised some particulars. Also, the actual talking document from which this was drawn was ten pages long. Consider this a small sample. If it helps, fine. If it doesn't, make yours do the job it needs to do for you.

Dear X:

Like I told you on the phone, a friend asked that I write a guest post for her blog about social media. Although I've been a professional writer for a decade and a half, I wouldn't consider myself a social media maven. I'm not sure what to write my post about. I want to give her readers something they can use, but I don't want to pretend I have knowledge I don't have.

Since you're a social media sage, I'd like to run a few ideas by you. None of them is worked out fully. Most are strategies from my regular consulting business made to fit a social media context. It'll give you a sense of each through some exploratory writing.

What works? What doesn't? I'd be grateful for feedback.

Best,

Mark

PART THREE: GOING PUBLIC

The first post idea I'll call "Your A-strategy isn't your A-strategy if you won't execute on it." That's a phrase I use with clients. What's it mean?

Businesses call me when a marketing initiative they're trying isn't working. Maybe they've started a blog, a white paper series, a group of live publicity stunts, or one of a hundred other things.

When I study the situation, more often than not I see that they say they're executing on the initiative, but the effort they're putting in is sketchy. They're not following through, or the material they're trying to execute on is off-target for them.

I ask why they picked that particular failing strategy. A common answer: They say that they heard that it was a perfect strategy, an A-strategy, for getting word out about a company. Everyone is using it.

What they haven't taken into account, though, is their own disposition, talents, and resources. Their own readiness. Businesses are like individuals. What's perfect for one is awful for another.

There is no such thing as an objective "A-strategy." An A-strategy is only an A-strategy if you'll execute on it. If you don't have the desire, talent, or resources to fully execute, then your B- or C-strategy should be elevated to A-strategy status. Execute on the strategy you'll perform with gusto. Gusto matters. Excitement matters. Follow-through matters. Completion matters.

I'd argue that the field of social media started as a C-strategy. People couldn't afford the A-strategies of TV commercials and major print advertisements, so they turned to what they could actually do and enjoy. Writing blogs and e-books. Making budget videos.

Look at many of the videos going viral. Those are C-strategies elevated to A. The thinking behind them: "We don't have the money to shoot a 'real' commercial. We can't afford the professional camera, the lighting, the film stock, the crew, the ad firm to script it. But we can afford a Flip camera. So let's come up with an idea, shoot it, and see what happens."

142

I think this idea of going with the strategy you can passionately get behind isn't just for the medium. It's for content, too. I read a quote in **Trust Agents** that speaks to this idea. Chris and Julien quoted Gary Vaynerchuk: "If you know everything there is to know about the show **Perfect Strangers,** start blogging about that and embrace it like there's no tomorrow. If you live and breathe NASCAR, there's your subject matter."

Said differently: Don't write about a subject just because you think you should write about it. If it's not something in your heart, you'll likely do a bad job on it. Write instead about what you're passionate about—even if what you're passionate about seems marginal or inappropriate to some. Your knowledge, your love, your mania will carry the day.

Questions I still have about writing about this idea:

How can you tell an A-strategy from a C-strategy ahead of time? I mean, it's easy to say I'm going to stick with what I do well, but what if you're really sticking to it because you're scared of trying something new? What if you stick with something that works but you miss out on growing?

What if you're good at something that's obviously dated? Like, suppose you're the best buggy whip manufacturer in the world. Do you stay making buggy whips? Do you continue to manufacture them, while promoting the buggy whip lifestyle, and hope to attract like-minded people as customers?

The second post idea I'll call....

→ Points to Remember

- There's benefit in articulating what you're thinking and feeling, even when you're not 100 percent sure what you're thinking and feeling. There's benefit, too, in sharing your fledging thoughts.
- A talking document helps you give shape to your thoughts and share them.
- To create a talking document, you can use one of these two ways, or combine them: (1) Write a letter to a friend or colleague about what you're thinking; (2) assemble pieces of your freewriting as a collage.
- Make sure ahead of time that the person you're writing to wants and has time to read the document. Also, tell them the kind of feedback you'd like.

Try This: Contact a friend or colleague today, and ask them if you can send them a document that contains your raw thinking on a problem that's bothering you. When they agree, take a day or two to assemble a talking document, and fire it off.

Chapter 23

Help Others Do Their Best Thinking

I'm a positioning consultant. When a client hires me, something predictable happens a few days before our first session. The client calls and asks for "prework." They want me to send a questionnaire they can answer that dissects their company. Their hope: that their answers yield clues, making the initial session more productive.

I don't, however, assign prework. The reason: It wastes time. Theirs and mine.

When I started in the consulting field, I saw colleagues giving prework, so, not wanting to disappoint, I'd send clients a questionnaire. They'd spend hours answering it. I'd spend hours reading it. I can't ever remember learning anything or seeing any surprises. Not once. After a while, I realized why.

Clients seek out consultants like me because they're stuck. They're not only repeatedly thinking the same thoughts, they're also thinking like everyone else in their field, at least as it relates to their marketplace position. Their responses to my questionnaire simply demonstrate that.

Their answers say all the things I've already read on their site and their competitors' sites. It's flat, homogenized stuff. It's so polished that all the humanity and distinction have been removed. Even their answers about goals and contributions are rendered in cold bullet-pointed fragments.

Reading information at this level of thinking won't get us anywhere. What will get us somewhere is if my client can get knocked off-balance. In a sense, they've got to forget who they've become so they can remember who they are.

I force them into new territory through a variety of methods. One method, as you might have guessed, is freewriting. I get clients to write, and we use the results as talking points for our conversations.

I'll ease a client into using writing. We start by having a conversation. I'll ask an innocuous question, like "Who're your prospects?" We'll discuss standard things, like industries and the problems those industries face.

Then, I'll try steering the conversation to a more interesting place by asking them about their customers. Here, they come up with better information, because they're thinking about real people instead of categories. Still, it's not completely where we need to be.

We then go for fresh territory. I ask them, not about all their customers, but about the four or five best customers they've ever had. Who has made doing business a joy, a rush? I want details: names, faces, ages, places, stories, scenes, images, scraps of conversation.

Most clients haven't given thought to this special group. If they have, it's usually been limited to demographic and psychographic studies that sit in bound reports with elaborate graphs.

At times, my client won't know where to begin the search for this personal list of their best and brightest. I can see from their postures and facial expressions that their minds are circling the concept, looking for an opening. That's when I need to stop them from thinking so hard. I ask that they open their laptops, turn to a blank document, and listen as I explain an unusual ideation method.

I'm giving them ten minutes to write about the best customers they've ever had. But this writing is unlike most writing they've ever done. They needn't show it to me or anyone else. They won't be asked to read it aloud. They can, in fact, delete it as soon as we're through.

They're to write fast and continuously for the ten minutes. They're not to worry about spelling, punctuation, or grammar. They're not to worry about whether what they're writing is interesting or even helpful. They can start writing about the subject from any spot they want. They can freely diverge from it if the spirit hits them.

I demonstrate by typing into the air, narrating as I go:

OK, Levy wants me to talk about my all-time favorite customers. Should I try listing as many as I can, or should I jump in and talk about one? Start with one. Who?

Jane Lawler comes to mind. A great client. Why's she so great? I remember the time she defended my judgment to her superiors, because she believed in the work we were doing. After that, I'd go through walls for her. Knowing that she was so thoroughly on my side really helped focus me on the work. I'd start on it as soon as I woke up in the morning, and I'd work through lunch and dinner without realizing it.

So Jane is one. And who's two? Not Chris Vaughn. I hate that guy. Makes things so much harder than they need to be. But his boss, Dale Foley, is amazing. The reason I love Dale is....

After my little show, I hit my timer and they write. If they slow or stop, I get on them: "Keep going. Don't think in your head. Think on the page. Start typing curses if that helps you decide what to write next."

147

When the alarm sounds, I ask about the writing process itself, as well as the content the process generated. Was this speed-writing method helpful, or did it get in the way? Without reading directly from the document, what thoughts and images did it trigger?

Invariably, they talk about things that hadn't before occurred to them: how they loved one customer because she helped them land ten new customers, and how they adored another customer because he throws a party for them at the conclusion of each project.

Despite my counseling them not to read aloud from their documents, they do. Even professed nonwriters do. Until now, they've never written with abandon, and they're delighted by the ideas and turns of phrase it often produces. They're proud of their work. It's a mastery experience.

The rest of the day goes similarly. I ask questions, we talk. When the client stays on the surface, or tries to stretch but can't, I halt the conversation and get them writing. Sometimes they're to do a straightforward brain dump. Other times, I assign a perspective-twisting exercise, such as asking them to follow the consequences of a lie.

The point here is not to be afraid to introduce freewriting to others. It's a perfect tool when you're working one-on-one with a client or colleague, and it works just as well in groups. I've used it in conference rooms with small groups, retreats with larger groups, and from the stage while keynoting to an audience of five hundred.

The only thing you want to look out for is giving people room to write. If they're right on top of each other, they may hold back their most honest thinking, because they think a neighbor can peek at their screen or paper.

While we're on the subject of freewriting with others, let me tell you about a technique that shares the freewriting spirit, yet hardly uses writing at all. I learned it from *How to Have Kick-Ass Ideas,* by Chris Baréz-Brown. It's called "blurt it out."

You can use it with groups and even crowds, but I'll describe it as a one-on-one exercise.

Suppose you have a problem to solve or an opportunity to discuss. Find a trusted friend, and sit across from them with your kitchen timer.

Take seven minutes, and talk about the opportunity. Don't, however, talk in your normal calm, measured way. Instead, speak as rapidly as you can, don't stop except to catch your breath, and hold nothing back. Essentially, you're having a freewriting conversation.

While you speak, your friend listens and jots down any striking facts, stories, or ideas.

When the seven minutes is up, now it's their turn. They have three minutes to tell you what they heard. They're also free to add their own opinions and ideas. You jot down anything you find interesting.

At the end of three minutes, there's one more round. You now have two minutes to tell your friend what you heard and how you might use the information in thinking about the opportunity.

I love this technique and, as I've said, have used it with groups. The energy generated is exciting, as people talk continuously about something they hold dear.

The only thing you have to be careful about is teaming up participants. Competitors, obviously, shouldn't be seated together. It's also not a good idea to pair employees with their immediate supervisor (the dynamic could be weird). I've found this works best when people from different industries work together. That way, a completely fresh pair of eyes is at work on the problem.

→ Points to Remember

- Teach freewriting to a client, a colleague, a team, an audience. Don't, however, just teach it as an intriguing skill. Teach

149

it to them as a means to open up thinking about a specific problem.

- Let people's freewriting stay private if they wish. Make sure they know they won't have to read from it unless they'd like to.

Chapter 24

Notice Stories Everywhere

When I interview people for a project, I try asking questions that can be answered with a story. Stories get at what's significant and raw. They're a main line to that part of our consciousness that hasn't yet sanitized memories.

Some of us are better than others at recalling stories. One of my favorite storytellers is John Vorhaus, a writer of mystery novels, books on writing technique, and manuals on how to win at poker. During an interview, I asked him for tales that in some way deal with writing. Here's a smattering of what he said:

Story #1
A large envelope arrived in the mail. I opened it and turned it over. Pieces of my book, *The Comic Toolbox*, came sliding out. So did a letter. The guy who sent it said the only value he got from my book came from ripping it up.

PART THREE: GOING PUBLIC

Not everyone will have a great relationship with what you write. That's the part you can't control. You just have to accept it. But there is something you can control: your part of the relationship, which is the writing of your book.

Story #2
I was at a street fair, seated at a table with a stack of my books for sale. No one was paying me attention. I didn't want to just sit there, so I started asking passersby, "What's the most important thing you know?" One guy said he thought that was the greatest pickup line he'd ever heard. I remembered that. Six months later I was at a wine tasting and used that line to meet the woman who would eventually become my wife.

Vorhaus told me a dozen stories. Did he have all these anecdotes cued up, knowing I'd ask for them during the interview? No, I hadn't prepared him. He was pulling them from memory on the fly. His engaging performance reminded me of what Lou Willett Stanek wrote: "Stories only happen to people who can tell them."

See, most of us go through our day and don't come away with a single story. Why? We don't need to. Creating and remembering a story doesn't contribute to anything we produce.

Vorhaus, on the other hand, is a writer, and he needs material to write about. His brain soaks up interesting phenomena as he goes about his life, because he never knows when he'll need it. He converts those phenomena into stories.

Not all the work of writing, then, happens at the computer or by pen. Much of it happens while we're opening envelopes and hitting on potential mates. Knowing that you have to write keeps you attentive and creative throughout the day. Life becomes your material.

Bloggers know this lesson well. David Meerman Scott, who writes three blog posts a week in addition to his books, e-books, videos, audios, and keynotes, told me nothing in his life goes to waste. It's all fodder for the stories that appear in his writing projects.

"I was in Logan Airport," he said, "and everywhere I went, music was blaring over the loudspeakers. The airport thinks they're doing people a service, but it's irritating. These days, no one needs music piped in. We have MP3 players, computers, PDAs. We're on the phone doing business. We don't want to yell over noise. That's a post. Sitting in the airport and hearing music we didn't choose to listen to is a post."

Andy Orrock, who blogs about payment-processing systems, focuses more narrowly on the problems he commonly faces in designing and running such systems. Says Orrock:

> I get my company's daily life down onto paper. If something is interesting to us, we figure people facing similar problems will find it interesting, too. My writing formula is something like, "Here's a problem.... Here's what I found out about it.... Here's what I did as a result...." Readers think, "This company really understands what I'm going through." They respect that.

Orrock, in fact, tries to write about as many types of system problems as possible. That way, the hit rate for finding his blog goes up.

If I'm making this collecting of stories and material seem like it's all irritation- and problem-focused, I don't mean to. Another part of life to pay attention to is the uplifting.

Kate Purmal has a degree in advanced mathematics and has spent her life as a C-level technology executive and management consultant. Because of her work and background, she was bottom-line focused. When she learned freewriting, though, it gave her a way to translate the other parts of her life into something that could be shared. A single story acted as the lightning rod for her change in thinking.

PART THREE: GOING PUBLIC

Purmal and her children were in their backyard when they noticed Bella, their six-pound gray-and-orange tabby, climbing a tree. The cat had her sights set on a hawk—twice her size—perched on a high branch.

As Bella inched closer, the bird swooped down at the cat, talons first. Bella retreated to a hard-to-reach part of the tree. When the hawk landed, Bella again stalked it. The back-and-forth battle lasted several minutes. Eventually, Bella withdrew to the house, and the hawk, minus a few feathers, flew off.

Purmal was so impressed by her petite cat's tenacity that she decided to write about it. That is something she wouldn't have done before. Says Purmal:

> Normally, I'd have been embarrassed to write that story, because it wasn't about business. But, for some reason, I knew it was important, it was something I had to write about, and the abandon of freewriting gave me confidence. I shared what I wrote with friends, who appreciated it. I then started blogging. I write about business and technology, but I also write about scenes like "Bella and the Hawk" that move me.

As you go about your day, then, keep your eyes open for stories and other kinds of material to use in your writing. At first you may not recognize something as worthy of writing about. But remember: If a story or a detail or an observation is interesting to you, then it'll probably be interesting to members of your audience. We are more alike than we are different.

And if you're not sure that you have enough material to be a writer, my advice to you is this: Start writing, regularly. As you freewrite day after day, you'll gain material as you go. Some of that material, some of those stories, will be created on the page. Other material, other stories, will be created without effort as you lead your life.

→ Points to Remember

- As you start to write for the public, your mind will change. You'll start seeing the world as stories and material. You'll pay more attention to what's happening around you.

Try This: Tell four stories during your next freewriting session.

Chapter 25

Build an Inventory of Thoughts

In the past few years, I've made it a habit to write regularly. Some of the things I write find their way into books, posts, and articles immediately. But as you can imagine, much of my writing is done to clarify my thinking. Private writing. It's not meant for publication, at least not right away.

Instead of deleting this exploratory writing, though, I use it as fuel for future public writing. Here's how:

The first thing I do is read over my freewriting and see if there's anything I want to save. I'm looking for ideas, observations, stories, and hypotheses. For want of a better phrase, I call each one of these a thought chunk.

When I find a promising chunk, I cut it out of the freewriting document and drop it into a separate document that holds similarly themed chunks. For instance, if the chunk pertains to positioning, I drop it in a previously created document called "Positioning." If the chunk deals with a publicity stunt, I drop it into a document called "Publicity Stunts." I have a document for every subject I commonly write about. They have no-frills titles like "Marketing Strategy," "Customer Experience," "Sales," "Live Presentations," "Writing Technique," "Sports," "Jokes," "Childhood," and "Pets." Each document contains dozens, even hundreds, of chunks on a single topic.

These chunks, by the way, aren't mere fragments. They're complete thoughts. That's what makes this method work. If I read a chunk even a decade from now, it would make sense to me. For example, from my "Positioning" document:

> Many of us tense up when asked to talk about our business in a sentence or two. But we already know how to do it perfectly. It's like talking about a movie. If someone asked about a movie you just saw, you wouldn't recount every scene. You'd pick something distinctive. "It's about a robot that travels back in time to protect its inventor." "It's a documentary about the beginnings of extreme skateboarding." "It's the new Daniel Day-Lewis film." Talking about your business is no different than talking about a movie.

From my "Sales" document:

> The best way to prove your claims is by offering a sample of your product or service. If you're selling peanuts, offer a free bag. If you're selling software, offer a sixty-day trial. If you're a productivity consultant, suggest a tip tailored to your prospect. You must give people a risk-free chance to test for themselves the very thing you're selling; otherwise, they'll think that they're somehow different from everyone else and your product or service won't work for them.

From my "Writing Technique" document:

> I read something by Donald Murray that struck me. He said if he got a top-paying assignment, he would get it done in the following way: four weeks of research, two hours of writing, and two weeks of rewriting. That's wild. In his overall process, writing the first draft is a micro-step.

From my "Live Presentation" document:

I read a great icebreaker for groups. The preparation: Buy a beach ball and use a thick black marker to cover the ball with a hundred fun or edgy questions. Some examples: "Who is one person you wish you never met?" "What is it about you that people find irresistible?" "What latest trend simply baffles you?" At the meeting: Stand everyone in a circle and randomly toss the ball. Whoever catches it announces their name and answers the question closest to their left thumb. They throw the ball to someone else. Everyone gets a turn. An aesthetic note: I'd write the questions in different sizes and at different angles. Looks more artsy that way.

From my "Childhood" document:

I remember, when I was five or six, running home from the supermarket with a box of Apple Jacks that had some awesome toy inside. A space ship? A soldier? I don't remember. Anyway, I went into the kitchen, found the big silver pot with black handles that mom made goulash in, and dumped in the entire contents of the cereal box. I figured it'd be easy to find the toy. I was mistaken. There was no toy. You had to collect and send proof of purchase seals. I didn't buy another box of Apple Jacks for twenty years.

Now, when a project comes up, I dip into the appropriate document and I'm in chunk heaven. Hundreds to choose from. Sometimes I use one as is and drop it into a new piece of writing I'm working on. Other times I'll revise it, or I'll stitch together several chunks and use those. I'll also use chunks as thought-starters for exploratory writing.

In essence, I'm keeping an inventory of thoughts on my computer. I'm stockpiling ideas, stories, and prose before I need them. When I dip into these documents and find the perfect chunks, it feels like cheating. Since I'm copying off myself, I get over it quickly.

Using this method will help you write faster with fewer headaches. It'll also help you write truer. You'll be using material you had time to think about. It won't be stuff you forced out because you couldn't think of anything better.

PART THREE: GOING PUBLIC

A few more thoughts about using thought chunks:

Keeping an organized inventory of thoughts is different from saying, "I've got ideas scattered throughout my computer. I'll search when the time comes." Therein lies madness. You'll feel pressured, and 90 percent of the time your search will come up empty. By saving and organizing chunks as you go, you're tending your lawn regularly so it's always thick and green.

An added benefit of this chunk approach: You'll remember your ideas and stories better. The material will be more actively stored in your brain, because you'll be paying more attention to it and will make judgments about it as you move it into documents.

At times a chunk won't neatly fit a single category. That's no problem. Cross-index it by dropping duplicates in as many documents as you wish.

As I'm combing through a document and come across a chunk, I ask myself two questions: (1) "How does this particular chunk relate to the subject I'm writing about?" and (2) "What subject can I write about based on this chunk?" Make sense? The chunk either supports something I'm in the process of writing, or I think about what new piece I could write, starting from that chunk.

When you examine your freewriting, think twice about discarding a chunk that appears mundane. Things that seem commonplace today can turn out to be gold tomorrow. For example, I used to do positioning intuitively until I decided to codify my methods. Fortunately, I'd kept the freewriting I'd do while positioning clients, even though lots of the concepts seemed obvious to me at the time. When I started reading through this writing, I saw insights I'd forgotten about, and they helped me create a strong process.

I fear I'm giving the impression that this chunk methodology is dependent on freewriting. It's not, of course. Freewriting at times doesn't even enter into it. Sometimes I'll get an idea while driving, and I'll type it directly into the proper document when I get a chance. Or I'll write an article that doesn't work, so I'll cut it up into chunks that I file. Any interesting idea should go into your files, no matter how the idea comes to you.

A last thought: The chunks I keep in my documents tend to be small: a few sentences to three quarters of a page long. But really, chunks can be of any size. They can even be dozens of pages long. I say this because of a conversation I had in 1997 with Ray Bradbury. Bradbury's breakthrough book was *Martian Chronicles*, which the author considered "an accidental novel." Why accidental? Bradbury hadn't set out to write a book. Instead, he was writing and publishing individual short stories. An editor, Walter Bradbury (no relation), saw many of these stories and gave the writer the idea to situate them on Mars and release the batch as a novel. Ray Bradbury never forgot the lesson. Later, he combined other short stories into the book *Dandelion Wine,* and he put together ideas from his stories, poems, and plays to form the book *Green Shadows, White Whale.* For Bradbury, then, his thought chunks were story-sized. He used them as building blocks to create new works. Don't limit yourself when you look at your own work. Consider how small chunks can fit together as well as much larger ones.

→ Points to Remember

- Why toss your writing when it can help you down the line? Cut your freewriting into thought chunks, and toss each chunk in an appropriately named document on your computer.
- Use a chunk in one of two ways: (1) as an addition to something you're working on or (2) as a thought-starter for brand-new work.

Try This:　Right now, take an hour to comb through your writing and start making your own thought chunk documents around the themes you most commonly write about.

Chapter 26

Write Your Own Rules

Hemingway couldn't just sit down and write cold. He needed writing rules—crutches—that he could lean on for support.

One of his rules involved a word quota. He gave himself the task of writing between 500 and 1,000 words a day, no matter how he felt or how the work was coming. He even recorded his totals on a wall chart. Another one of his rules involved stopping the day's writing in mid-sentence. The famed author's last thought would sit incomplete until the next writing session.

Word quotas and unfinished sentences? Why did Hemingway use these gimmicks?

Even for Hemingway, facing the page could be daunting. The right word or plot point could be painfully elusive. Knowing, however, how the session would begin ("I have to complete yesterday's sentence") and conclude ("I can stop anywhere between 500 and 1,000 words") gave him the confidence to face the uncertainty of writing.

Hemingway, of course, was not alone in his need for writing rules. We're all better off if we can approach the page knowing what to do and knowing we can do it.

When I haven't planned my writing day, I hesitate starting at all. I'll roughhouse with the dogs, answer e-mail, and empty the dishwasher. Putting off writing isn't a conscious thing. A subliminal spinelessness kicks in. At times, the day will pass without my writing a word.

When I'm in my right mind, I know how to bypass the hesitation before it takes hold. Like Hemingway, I give myself rules. I usually decide on the rules the night before. What kind of rules depends on what I'm trying to accomplish.

If I decide to ease into writing, my rules are like a hurdler's stretches. I'm not trying to do much other than loosen up.

One of the warm-ups I use might be called the opposites game. I read about the concept in John Vorhaus's *The Comic Toolbox*. It was created to help people write sitcoms and other comedic work. The rules take some explaining, but playing it is simple and fun.

First, write down a person, place, or thing. You needn't be too imaginative here. Conventional stuff works fine.

Second, convert that person, place, or thing into its opposite. What do I mean? Say you initially wrote "black cat." What might its opposite be? Since black cats have no true agreed-upon opposite, you can choose from lots of possibilities. "White" could be considered an opposite of black. "Dog" could be considered an opposite of cat. So, "white dog" could fit as an opposite of black cat.

But you could also play off the popular superstition: If a black cat is bad luck, your black cat is opposed to that: Yours is good luck. That's what you'd write: "A black cat that's lucky."

Suppose you next wrote "skunk." What do people associate with skunks? A rank, consuming odor. How, then, might your skunk be opposed to that association? Yours smells good. Or even better, yours shoots perfume. You might write down "A skunk that sprays Chanel #5."

You'd keep on going, writing down words and converting them into literal or loosely defined opposites. Some more examples:

A politician who is afraid of public speaking

A comedian who tells only straight lines

A mechanic who works in a tuxedo

A sore throat that helps you sleep through the night

A tissue made from sandpaper

A hammer blown from glass

A computer keyboard with unmarked keys

A fish that mustn't get wet

A raisin that rehydrates into a grape

Lasagna stuffed with prunes

A cloud that rains kerosene

A country without a flag

An economy based on flaxseed

Again, there's a lot of leeway as to what's considered an opposite. Take the last example, "an economy based on flaxseed." Until the early 1970s, most economies were based on the gold standard, so that's the concept I was subverting. Is flaxseed the opposite of gold? That's one possibility. Gold is a hard metal with tremendous monetary value, while flaxseed is plant material that, in comparison, is almost worthless. For me, that's a fit. At least as a warm-up.

Notice, too, that the more specific the word choices are, the more interesting the opposites become. Since most lasagna is stuffed with meat or vegetables, one stuffed with fruit would have qualified as an opposite. However, one stuffed with prunes makes the image more visceral.

When playing the opposites game, I give myself a twenty-minute limit. Otherwise, I might play it all day. It forces you to see things differently, with a smile.

Once I'm warm, I go into my real work. That, too, has rules I can follow without hassle.

If I'm doing ideation work, one of the rules I might give myself is to first brainstorm, not my problem's solutions, but all the questions that spring to mind when I consider it. Why do I brainstorm questions?

Trying to come up with solutions can be nerve-racking. There's too much room for thinking things like "These solutions are horrible. I've lost whatever brains I ever had. I'll never find an answer." Brainstorming questions, though, is easy. You can't do it wrong.

What kinds of questions do I brainstorm? Every possible kind from every possible angle, rapid-fire. No thinking.

Suppose I wanted to come up with a marketing campaign for a product. What kinds of questions would I ask?

What's the product do?

Why was it invented?

How is it better than anything else out there?

How is it worse?

Who might buy it?

Why might they buy it?

Why might they ignore it?

Why might they hate it?

Why might they love it?

How might they find out about it?

How might word spread?

How might they buy it?

What might they be doing five minutes before buying it?

How is it packaged?

What's the business model?

Where's the inventory?

How fast can it be made?

How much does it cost to make?

How would it be shipped?

What might the guarantee be?

How would returns be handled?

What resources do we have?

What resources don't we have?

What are the worst things we can do in marketing this product?

What are the best things we can do in marketing this product?

What concerns me most here?

What concerns me least?

If I took twenty minutes, I'd probably come up with a hundred or more questions. Once I'd gotten them out of my head and onto paper, I could decide which, if any, should be answered.

If I have rules for warming up and ideating, you'd better believe I have rules for writing prose, too. Lots of them.

One of my prose rules has to do with keeping the writing step and the revising step separate. When you try to write and edit at the same time, you overwhelm yourself. David Taylor calls this unfortunate situation "task overload." The term makes instant sense. Generating prose is one task. Making prose sound good is a second task. Trying to do them simultaneously gives your brain too much to do. In response, your brain locks like a computer that's been given excessive and contradictory commands.

I remind myself, then: Stay away from task overload. You can do only one thing at a time. Generate ideas and prose first. Generate too much stuff, in the wrong words. Once you've done that, then decide which things you should keep, which you should chuck, and how to make things sound better.

A few final thoughts about rules:

The big idea I want to convey here is that you should just sit down and starting writing if that's an approach that regularly works for you. If it doesn't, however, try giving yourself a rule or two to guide your thinking and behavior. Having rules will get you writing and keep you writing. You won't continually ask yourself, "What do I do now?"

A rule can be a number of things, including an exercise to try, a technique to follow, an assignment to complete, a piece of philosophy that guides you, or a design parameter that supports you. Your rule, though, needs to be actionable and measurable. Its job is not primarily to make you feel confident or calm. A good rule helps you write.

The rules you use should be uncomplicated. They should be things you know you can pull off (although whether you do a good job during any particular session is another story). Telling yourself to outline can be a good rule. Telling yourself that you're going to experiment by writing in the second person can be a good rule. Telling yourself that you'll have five raw versions of your opening paragraph by the end of the day's writing could be a good rule. Demanding that your day's writing must change your life is a bad rule.

By all means, create your own rules. A rule is a way of narrowing your focus to something concrete and doable. While we're following a rule, we can accomplish other things as a result. Suppose, for instance, that you're on deadline to write a blog post about financial management. You decide to turn your writing into a game by giving yourself a rule: You're somehow going to fit the words "mayonnaise," "wiper blades," and "Mars" into your writing. That's an arbitrary but potentially good rule, because you'll probably complete your post while following it.

→ Points to Remember

- Before approaching your day's writing, give yourself some uncomplicated, easy-to-do rules to follow. Doing so will focus you.
- Different parts of the creative process call for different rules. You can create a warm-up rule, an ideation rule, a writing rule, and so forth. Don't, however, weigh yourself down with rules. Their sole purpose is to help you. A good rule enables you to get the job done.

Try This: Come up with one writing rule, and try it out now. If you can't think of one, use this: Freewrite about a problem by listing bad solutions: one lousy, stupid, improbable, embarrassing, obnoxious, or dangerous idea after another.

Chapter 27

The Fascination Method

One of the hats I wear is that of writing coach. I guide businesspeople in writing books. During a typical first session, my clients aren't sure what their book will be about, but they take guesses. They tell me what they think the marketplace wants and what they believe they can sell. They start tossing around promising premises. I stop them.

Books indeed need readers, so thinking about audience is important. Books also help writers achieve career goals, so thinking strategically about how a book can advance one's business makes sense, too. But looking at those things too early leads to a bland book.

Writers start misplacing their attention. Instead of focusing on the best things they've learned and on telling readers what they need to hear, writers try to read minds so they can give the market exactly what it expects and approves of.

The situation reminds me of a scene from the American version of the sitcom *The Office*. When Andy is transferred, he tries to curry favor with his new boss, Michael, by subtly imitating Michael's word choices and speaking cadence. At first Michael likes him, because he and Andy seem oddly similar. After a while, though, Andy's parroting becomes a nuisance because he won't make a decision on his own and is always waiting to follow Michael's lead.

On *The Office,* this yes-man dynamic is funny. In real life, it's sad. If you want to write a book that's at all original, that's at all valuable, that's at all like you at your best, you need to adopt a leadership position.

As Eric Maisel says, writing a book creates meaning. You're bringing something into the world that doesn't yet exist. You get to decide what fits and what doesn't.

Think of yourself as a filter. As you've moved through the world, you've had millions of experiences and collected ideas, stories, and memories unique to you. It's from that storehouse of meaning inside your head where your book should begin. By using some of these collected phenomena bubbling in your head, you will have a book that has your stamp on it and is unlike any other.

When I'm working with clients, I tell them to temporarily put aside considerations of others and of worldly success, and I ask that they make a list. What kind of list? It's an inventory of everything that fascinates or has fascinated them at any point in their lives. I'm talking a list of:

- facts
- figures
- insights
- prejudices
- anecdotes
- pet philosophies
- experiences
- case studies
- controversies
- analogies
- processes
- methods
- hypotheses
- risks

- surprises
- memories
- business models
- role models
- URLs
- blogs
- scenes
- dreams
- screwy notions
- poems
- jokes
- riddles
- myths
- trips

- conversations
- art
- plays
- books
- movies
- TV shows

Anything makes the list that the client thinks should make the list, good or bad, big or small, important or trivial. They're not to wonder why a particular item fascinates them. They're not to worry if an item is book-worthy, or has anything to do with their core business. Their task is to list items that, for whatever reason, have energy for them. Items that radiate.

What we're doing is playing a game: We're treating anything that appears in the client's mind as potentially valuable book material.

They can compose the list through any methods they please. I advise them to use a combination of freewriting sessions and plain old daydreaming, spread over the course of days. Once they've made their list, only then do we start thinking about would-be readers and business goals.

Who might the audience be? How are they different from the rest of the population? What is the client qualified to talk to them about? What kinds of things does that audience need to hear? What's the most important thing they need to hear? What kinds of solutions would they be most eager to buy from the client? What solutions would bring the client closest to their personal and business goals? What kind of book stands the best chance of getting everyone exactly what they want? What book demands to be written?

After discussing all that information, we study the fascinations list, move items around, add to them, group them, and look for themes. Believe me, we find themes. It's like what Edward Tufte meant when he wrote that "the act of arranging information becomes an act of insight." We get new ideas just by recombining what's in front of us.

From these places of energy, we find the book's premise and much of its supporting material. This material comes from an honest place within the client. It comes from the spot in their brain where they keep things they can't forget.

Using this fascination method, everyone gets a fair hearing: the client as meaning maker, the client as businessperson, and the reading audience.

Now, the writing can begin. The resulting book will stand a better chance of being something readers can use and a book that's uniquely the writer's.

By the way, this production method isn't only for book writing. Any storyteller can use it, no matter what the medium. The key is to generate lots of material so you can cut the filler and use the parts with juice.

→ Points to Remember

- When you want to write something important, don't look to the market first. The market will force you into a thousand directions if you let it. Instead, look to your fascinations, the things you love and can't forget about life. Take an inventory.
- From this inventory, look for themes and material that particularly excite you. Only then should you consider the market.
- Use this rich combination of personal material and audience focus to create a one-of-a-kind document.

Chapter 28

Freewrite Your Way to Finished Prose

Geoff Bellman, author of *The Consultant's Calling* and *Your Signature Path*, is a thoughtful business writer. I asked him how he goes about writing a book. He said his books don't start as books. They begin as explorations. You could say he freewrites his way into them.

When Bellman first sits down to write, he uses the time to learn what he's thinking about without having to explain himself to other people. He doesn't want to use the page as a means of persuading others, making money, or making himself famous. When they are addressed too early, he sees those factors as corrupting forces. They get in the way of developing meaningful work.

During a writing session, which lasts about four hours, Bellman lets his ideas pull him forward. He sets a topic in mind, like "consulting" or "organizations," and has conversations with himself on the page. He follows side trails, doesn't worry about style, doesn't edit, and doesn't look back at what he's written. When he's produced ten double-spaced pages, the day's session is over.

After four to six weeks of sessions, he's produced 200 to 300 pages. He prints them out, reads them, and asks himself, "What am I saying here? What's useful to me? What's useful to other people? What's crap?"

If Bellman thinks he has something important to say, he considers turning his work into a manuscript. He'll go through the raw writing, whose concepts he sees as bones. "Of course, I don't want to give readers a pile of bones," he says, so he assembles them into the book's skeleton. He decides which concepts are most important and which fulfill a structural role.

Bellman sits back and takes a look at his creation. He asks himself, "Am I attached enough to the concept to flesh it out?" If the answer is yes, he'll add to it and polish it. If not, he'll discard it.

Bellman even uses the writing-as-thinking process when working with a coauthor. Writing *Extraordinary Groups* is a perfect example. He and his colleague, Kathleen Ryan, discussed collaborating on a book. They knew it would be about groups, but they weren't sure of much else. Ryan started conducting studies to ferret out ideas and stories to include in the possible book. Bellman devoted his time to exploratory writing. "I wanted to know what I thought before I heard what others thought," said Bellman. After a hundred or so pages, his material convinced him that there was something to share with an audience.

I approach writing books and articles in much the same way as Bellman. I start by exploring, although my search is not endless. It follows steps and time limits.

Suppose I want to write an article. The first thing I might do is warm up with ten minutes of freewriting and fast exercises. Maybe two or three of them. For the most part, I steer clear of business ideas. I'm writing about a world event that has my attention, a dream I had, a story I remembered, a TV show I watched. I may play the opposites game (Chapter 26) or follow a writing prompt (Chapter 8).

Once I'm warm, I do about a half-dozen focused freewriting sessions on the article topic. I dump everything I know about the subject onto the page, and I also force my mind in new directions. I'm courting surprise. Here's where I'll open up words, list bad ideas, have paper conversations, and the like.

Understand, I'm not trying to write the article yet. There's no flowing narrative. I'm working in ideas. I'm a child playing in mud. If good prose comes out of this, that's a bonus, but I don't expect it.

When I'm finished doing this focused freewriting, I read it over and separate the dead from the living. The dead stuff—babble, off-point notions, wrong-headed thinking—I delete or save to other documents for use in a future project (Chapter 25). The living stuff—on-point ideas, interesting turns of phrase, experiments that could stand further pursuit—I arrange in a provisional order that seems to make sense. Let's call this result my master document.

At this point, I want a clear picture of what I have in my master document and what I still might need to add. To get this picture, I take a pad and pen and comb through my on-screen work. For each chunk of prose I read, I sum it up on the pad in a sentence.

If I was writing an article on elevator speeches and I wrote this chunk:

You're embarrassed. When people ask you what you do for a living, you don't know what to say. Naturally, you know what you do and you do a damn good job at it, but somehow when you blurt it out it seems like a corruption of who you are. You're so much more than that. It goes beyond embarrassment. Not knowing how to articulate who you are and what you do, in a way that's clear and excites, is costing you money and a sense of direction for your business.

I might turn it into this sentence: "Not knowing how to talk about your business is embarrassing, and is costing you in terms of money and direction."

Once I had all these sentence-long summations on my pad, I'd read through them to see what still needed saying. I'd write down as a sentence in the appropriate spot anything that came to mind.

When I was finished, of course, what I'd have is an outline. It would be an outline based on concepts I've actively thought about, not concepts listed out of obligation.

Based on the outline, I'd start creating a first draft. What would that entail? I'd probably do some freewriting on the concepts I missed during my first series of sessions, and I'd plug the best parts of those into the master document. I'd then continue on, rewriting, cutting, and polishing as needed.

I try not to get too concerned about or devote too much time to any particular draft. A colleague of mine, Barry Tarshis, calls this approach taking passes at the material. I work on the document for a while; then I leave it and work on something else. I come back minutes, hours, or even days later, and take another pass at it. Over and over the cycle goes. The advantage of taking passes: Each time you approach the document, you're more likely to see it with fresh eyes and renewed enthusiasm. You're less likely to be blinded by what has become invisible to you because you've been staring at it for so long.

When might I finish the article? My smart aleck answer: It depends. It depends on how many words long the piece needs to be, how much extra research I need to do, and what else I have on my plate. No piece is ever truly finished. Changes can always be made. Even the greats of literature continually made edits if you let them. Walt Whitman released six different editions of *Leaves of Grass.* When Dylan Thomas read on stage, he'd edit his own work on the fly, and passages of Shakespeare's, too.

To know when I'm finished, the biggest piece of information I need is the deadline. I ask the person who assigned the article, "When do you need it by?" If they need it by Wednesday, I give them Wednesday's version. If they need it by next Friday, I give them next Friday's version. Will next Friday's version be better than this Wednesday's version, because I've had more time to work on it? I'd like to think so, but that's not necessarily true. For all I know, I may unintentionally do damage to the article if I'm given more time. Writing is a funny game.

→ Points to Remember

- Freewriting is a freestyle thinking technique that ignores conventional writing rules and courts surprise. Nevertheless, you can use it as a tool for creating finished prose.
- One way of using freewriting to create finished prose: Do a series of freewriting warm-ups. Then, do more focused freewriting about the topic that's meaningful to you. Cut away what's not working, arrange the remaining pieces in a provisional order, and make an outline so you know what you have to work with. Write any missing ideas and transitions. Edit. Edit. Edit. Tah-da! A finished piece.
- Revisit your finished piece as much as you'd like, but know that it can never truly be finished. Get "Wednesday's Version" out the door by Wednesday.

Try This:　Mark Bowden said a writer should always be working on the most ambitious thing he or she has ever done. What writing project would most stretch and excite you? Start now by using freewriting to help you.

Notes

Opening Quote

Clouse, Barbara Fine. *Working It Out: A Troubleshooting Guide for Writers*. New York: McGraw-Hill, 1993. p. 17.

Chapter 1. Try Easy

Kriegel, Robert J., and Louis Patler. *If It Ain't Broke... Break IT!— and Other Unconventional Wisdom for a Changing Business World*. New York: Warner Books, 1991. p. 61.

Chapter 2. Write Fast and Continuously

Bradbury, Ray. *Zen in the Art of Writing: Releasing the Creative Genius within You*. New York: Bantam Books, 1990. p. 13.

Chapter 3. Work against a Limit

Palahniuk, Chuck. "13 Writing Tips" at http://chuckpalahniuk. net/workshop/essays/chuck-palahniuk.

Chapter 4. Write the Way You Think

Macrorie, Ken. *Writing to Be Read*, Revised Third Edition. Portsmouth, NH: Heinemann, 2006. pp. 207–213.

Notes

Chapter 9. Open Up Words

Owen, Harrison. *Expanding Our Now: The Story of Open Space Technology.* San Francisco: Berrett-Koehler, 1997. pp. 69–70.

Chapter 10. Escape Your Own Intelligence

Macrorie, Ken. *Telling Writing,* Fourth Edition. Portsmouth, N.H.: Heinemann, 1985. p. 45.

Chapter 11. The Value in Disconnecting

Schneider, Pat. *The Writer as an Artist: A New Approach to Writing Alone and with Others.* Los Angeles: Lowell House, 1994. p. 14.

Hugo, Richard. *The Triggering Town: Lectures and Essays on Poetry and Writing.* New York: W. W. Norton, 1979. p. 4.

Chapter 13. Getting a Hundred Ideas Is Easier Than Getting One

Stafford, William. *Writing the Australian Crawl: Views on the Writer's Vocation.* Ann Arbor: University of Michigan Press, 1978. p. 18.

Murray, Donald. *Writing for Your Readers: Notes on the Writer's Craft from the* Boston Globe, Second Edition. Old Saybrook, CT: Globe Pequot Press, 1992. p. 66. Murray says *he* would write fifty to seventy-five leads for a magazine article, although I met a reporter who worked with him and said he taught the idea to students as well.

Chapter 16. Drop Your Mind on Paper

Schank, Roger, with Peter Childers. *The Creative Attitude: Learning to Ask and Answer the Right Questions.* New York: Macmillan, 1988. pp. 91–126.

Chapter 17. The Writing Marathon

Bradbury, Ray. *Zen in the Art of Writing: Releasing the Creative Genius within You.* New York: Bantam Books, 1990. p. 13.

Carlson, Ron. *Ron Carlson Writes a Story.* Saint Paul, MN: Graywolf Press, 2007. p. 15.

Messer, Mari. *Pencil Dancing: New Ways to Free Your Creative Spirit.* Cincinnati: Walking Stick Press, 2001. p. 37. (I first saw the term "writing marathon" coined in this book.)Elbow, Peter. *Writing With Power: Techniques for Mastering the Writing Process.* New York: Oxford University Press, 1981. p. 59.

Notes

Poets.org calls "Make it new!" Pounds' "battle cry." See http://www.poets.org/viewmedia.php/prmMID/5664

Chapter 18. Doubt Yourself

Whyte, David. Drawn from an interview with the author.

Chapter 19. The Magic of Exact Writing

Wolfe, Tom. *The Kandy-Kolored Tangerine-Flake Streamline Baby.* Reprinted edition. New York: Bantam, 1999. p. xii.

Elbow, Peter. *Writing with Power: Techniques for Mastering the Writing Process.* New York: Oxford University Press, 1981. p. 336.

Chapter 20. Extract Gold from a Business Book

Hudson, William J. *Intellectual Capital: How to Build It, Enhance It, Use It.* New York: John Wiley & Sons, 1993. p. 212.

Crosby, Philip. *The Absolutes of Leadership.* San Francisco: Jossey-Bass, 1996. p. 78.

Chapter 21. You Are What You Focus On

Bellman, Geoffrey M. *The Consultant's Calling—Bringing Who You Are to What You Do.* San Francisco: Jossey-Bass, 1990. p. 129.

Chapter 22. Sharing Your Unfinished Thoughts

Brogan, Chris, and Julien Smith. *Trust Agents: Using the Web To Build Influence, Improve Reputation, and Earn Trust.* Hoboken, NJ: John Wiley & Sons, 2009. p. 71.

Chapter 23. Help Others Do Their Best Thinking

Baréz-Brown, Chris. *How to Have Kick-Ass Ideas: Shake Up Your Business, Shake Up Your Life.* New York: Skyhorse Publishing, 2008. pp. 140–141.

Chapter 24. Notice Stories Everywhere

Vorhaus, John. Drawn from an interview with the author.

Stanek, Lou Willett. *So You Want to Write a Novel: A Direct, Practical, Step-by-Step Guide for the Aspiring Author.* New York: HarperCollins, 1994. p. ix.

Scott, David Meerman. Drawn from an interview with the author.

Orrock, Andy. Drawn from an interview with the author.

Purmal, Kate. Drawn from an interview with the author.

Notes

Chapter 25. Build an Inventory of Thoughts

For the icebreaker, see http://www.residentassistant.com/games/icebreakers/beachball.htm.

Bradbury, Ray. Drawn from a discussion with the author.

Chapter 26. Write Your Own Rules

Linscott, Roger Bourne. "On the Books." See http://www.timelesshemingway.com/faq/faq5.shtml.

Vorhaus, John. *The Comic Toolbox: How to Be Funny Even When You're Not.* Hollywood, CA: Silman-James Publishing, 1994. pp. 21–22.

Taylor, David. "Fighting Writer's Block – Part 1: Causes and Cures." http://www.writing-world.com/basics/block1.shtml.

Chapter 27. The Fascination Factor

NBC. *The Office*, Season 3, Episode 8: "The Merger."

Tufte, Edward. *Visual Explanations: Images and Quantities, Evidence and Narrative.* Cheshire, CT: Graphics Press, 1997. p. 9.

Maisel, Eric. *The Art of the Book Proposal: From Focused Idea to Finished Proposal.* New York: Tarcher, 2004. p. 8.

Chapter 28. Freewrite Your Way to Finished Prose

Bellman, Geoffrey M. Drawn from an interview with the author.

Whitman's many editions are discussed at http://www.whitmanarchive.org/published/LG/index.html.

For Mark Bowden, see Heidi Benson. "'Black Hawk' author found untold story" (SFGATE, February 09, 2003) at http://articles.sfgate.com/2003-02-09/books/17477347_1_atlantic-books-major-publisher-nonfiction.

Acknowledgments

While writing this book, I received spiritual and technical support from dozens of people. Here are only some of the wonderful folk who helped me: Stella, my lovely, genius wife; Rhoda, my amazing mom; Paul, my brilliant brother (and Lynda, Craig, and Camille); Joyce, my sensational sister; Gil Leffman, my astonishing uncle; the awesome Adelman clan; and Stella's extraordinary kin. In addition, Karl Weber, who agented and edited the original edition of this book with virtuosity; Steve Piersanti, who honored me by signing me up the first time; Johanna Vondeling, who honored me by signing me the second time and coached me with intelligence and enthusiasm; the ever-cool Berrett-Koehler staff; and Steve Cohen, for his friendship and brilliance.

I'd also like to send a huge "Thanks!" to the following folks: Marilee Adams; Dick and Emily Axelrod; Allan Bacon; Joel Bauer; Ron Bauer; Geoff Bellman; Matt Blair; Noah

Acknowledgments

Blumenthal; Ray Bradbury; Tom Clifford ("Cranberry sauce"); Jeff and Carol Cohen; Jerry "Northern Boulevard" Colonna; Nick Corcodilos; my friends at CRI; Charles Dorris; Alvin Eng (aka "my friend the editor" from the intro, whose deadline forced freewriting on me); Bob Farmer; Brendan "The Kid" Flaherty; Jack Foster; Jason Friedman (a force of nature); Michael Gelb; Nathan Gold; Steve Goldberg and my friends at Bookazine; Alan Greenberg; Cliff Hakim; Christina Harbridge (whose life embodies freewriting); CV Harquail; Paul Harris; Nettie Hartsock (who devotes her life to helping others and making contributions); Seth Harwood; Sally Helgesen; Gary Hoover; Sam Horn; Wayne Hurlbert; Jake Jacobs; Sharon Jordan Evans; Larina Kase (for being as excited about this book as I am, and for her expert help with the subtitle and cover); Lynn Kearney; Mary Key; Mac King; Mark Lefko; Paul Lemberg; Michelle Lennox; Eric Maisel; Jay Matalon; Joy Matkowski; Bill O'Hanlon (who didn't enjoy writing until his seventeenth book); Andy Orrock; Detta Penna; Tom Peters; Kate Purmal (who so loves freewriting she wants to teach it to everyone in the world); Jon Racherbaumer; Dr. David Reynolds; Becky Roemen and my EO friends; Adam Rubin; Steve Sanderson; Roger Schank; Rich Schefren; Doug Schrade ("I need your book!"); Allison Scott; David Meerman Scott (for his friendship and for proving you can be famous and a great guy at the same time); Claudio Sennhauser; Simon Sinek; Robyn Steely; Ken Swezey; Barry Tarshis (whose books helped make me a writer); my friends who helped on Twitter; Paul Van Slambrouck (for his Pulitzer-quality suggestions); Joe Vitale (for his friendship and his love of life); John Vorhaus; Debbie Weil; David Whyte; Leslie Yerkes; Cali Yost; and Glenn Young.

Also, a special thanks to Kuma, Jofu, Bea, Tiger, Jinx, and Betsy Levy.

And thank you, Peter Elbow, for writing your books.

Index

Index

Index

About Mark Levy

Christopher Barth

Mark Levy is the founder of Levy Innovation LLC (www. levyinnovation.com), a marketing strategy firm that helps consultants and entrepreneurial companies increase their fees by up to 2,000 percent.

Mark accomplishes that through positioning and by helping clients invent concepts around which they can base their entire businesses. He also coaches people on how to write books that become skyrockets for their businesses, and gives keynote speeches and workshops on ideation and freewriting.

David Meerman Scott calls Mark "a positioning guru extraordinaire" and Scott's own "guru on call." Joe Vitale calls Mark "a Superman of the Mind. He's a walking, talking, money-making brain on steroids. Computers want to grow up and be like him. And I'm probably underdescribing his abilities."

About Mark Levy

Before Levy Innovation, Mark was a director at a book wholesaler, where he helped sell a billion dollars worth of product and was nominated three times for the *Publishers Weekly* Rep of the Year Award.

Mark has written for the *New York Times* and has written or cocreated five books: *How to Persuade People Who Don't Want to Be Persuaded* (Wiley, 2005), *Accidental Genius: Revolutionize Your Thinking through Private Writing* (Berrett-Koehler, 2000), *Tricks with Your Head* (Crown, 2002), and *Magic for Dummies* (IDG, 1998). His work has been praised by Ray Bradbury, Tom Peters, Anthony Robbins, David Pogue, Al Ries, Jay Conrad Levinson, Gary Hoover, and Penn & Teller.

Mark has also taught research-based business writing at Rutgers University.

Since he was six years old, Mark has been interested in magic. The tricks he has invented have been performed in Las Vegas and on all the major TV networks. He cocreated the off-Broadway shows *Chamber Magic: A Demonstration of Modern Conjuring* and *Miracles at Midnight*. *Chamber Magic* is the longest-running one-man show in New York City.

E-mail Mark at mark@levyinnovation.com.

Berrett–Koehler Publishers

Berrett-Koehler is an independent publisher dedicated to an ambitious mission: *Creating a World That Works for All.*

We believe that to truly create a better world, action is needed at all levels—individual, organizational, and societal. At the individual level, our publications help people align their lives with their values and with their aspirations for a better world. At the organizational level, our publications promote progressive leadership and management practices, socially responsible approaches to business, and humane and effective organizations. At the societal level, our publications advance social and economic justice, shared prosperity, sustainability, and new solutions to national and global issues.

A major theme of our publications is "Opening Up New Space." Berrett-Koehler titles challenge conventional thinking, introduce new ideas, and foster positive change. Their common quest is changing the underlying beliefs, mindsets, institutions, and structures that keep generating the same cycles of problems, no matter who our leaders are or what improvement programs we adopt.

We strive to practice what we preach—to operate our publishing company in line with the ideas in our books. At the core of our approach is stewardship, which we define as a deep sense of responsibility to administer the company for the benefit of all of our "stakeholder" groups: authors, customers, employees, investors, service providers, and the communities and environment around us.

We are grateful to the thousands of readers, authors, and other friends of the company who consider themselves to be part of the "BK Community." We hope that you, too, will join us in our mission.

A BK Life Book

This book is part of our BK Life series. BK Life books change people's lives. They help individuals improve their lives in ways that are beneficial for the families, organizations, communities, nations, and world in which they live and work. To find out more, visit **www.bk-life.com**.

Berrett–Koehler Publishers

A community dedicated to creating
a world that works for all

Visit Our Website: www.bkconnection.com

Read book excerpts, see author videos and Internet movies, read our authors' blogs, join discussion groups, download book apps, find out about the BK Affiliate Network, browse subject-area libraries of books, get special discounts, and more!

Subscribe to Our Free E-Newsletter, the *BK Communiqué*

Be the first to hear about new publications, special discount offers, exclusive articles, news about bestsellers, and more! Get on the list for our free e-newsletter by going to **www.bkconnection.com**.

Get Quantity Discounts

Berrett-Koehler books are available at quantity discounts for orders of ten or more copies. Please call us toll-free at (800) 929-2929 or email us at bkp.orders@aidcvt.com.

Join the BK Community

BKcommunity.com is a virtual meeting place where people from around the world can engage with kindred spirits to create a world that works for all. **BKcommunity.com** members may create their own profiles, blog, start and participate in forums and discussion groups, post photos and videos, answer surveys, announce and register for upcoming events, and chat with others online in real time. Please join the conversation!

SUSTAINABLE FORESTRY INITIATIVE
Certified Fiber Sourcing
Label applies to the text stock
www.sfiprogram.org